The Story of the Middle Ages

Feudalism, the Church, Europe's Nations and the Crusades – A History of Medieval Times for Young Readers

By Samuel B. Harding

Published by Pantianos Classics

ISBN-13: 978-1-78987-246-0

First published in 1901

Contents

Preface

The point of view from which this book is written is perhaps suffi-
ciently set forth in the introductory chapter, but it may fittingly call for an
additional word in this place. It is, namely, the point of view of one who
believes that the child about to undertake the formal study of American
history in the seventh and eight grades of our schools, needs first a pre-
liminary sketch of the history of earlier times,—especially of the Middle
Ages,—in order that our own history may appear in its true perspective
and setting.

In attempting to make intelligible to children the institutions and
events of the Middle Ages, the author is aware of the magnitude of the
task which he has essayed. He is, however, firmly of the opinion that the
difficulty arises frequently not so much from an inability on the part of
the child to grasp the essential ideas underlying medieval relations, as
from the lack of a clear understanding of these on the part of the narrator
himself, and the need of finding familiar non-technical terms of definition.
Whether the difficulty has been entirely surmounted in this work can only be determined by the test of use; but at least no pains have been
spared in the effort.

The interest of the book, no doubt, might have been enhanced had the
author wished to give stories, instead of "the story" of the Middle Ages.
Detached episodes, striking figures, romantic tales, exist in plenty to rivet
the child's attention and fire his fancy; but it has been no part of the plan
of this work to draw attention to particular persons and events at the expense of the whole. "Somehow," writes Walter Bagehot of historical reading for children, "the whole comes in boyhood; the details later and in
manhood. The wonderful series going far back to the times of the old pa-
triarchs with their flocks and herds, the keen-eyed Greek, the stately Roman, the watching Jew, the uncouth Goth, the horrid Hun, the settled picture of the unchanging East, the restless shifting of the rapid West, the
rise of the cold and classical civilization, its fall, the rough impetuous
Middle Ages, the vague warm picture of ourselves and home,—when did
we learn these? Not yesterday nor to-day; but long ago in the first dawn
of reason, in the original flow of fancy. What we learn afterwards are but
the accurate littlenesses of the great topic, the dates and tedious facts.

Those who begin late learn only these; but the happy first feel the mystic associations and the progress of the whole."

July 1901

The opportunity afforded by the necessity of making new pages for the book has been used to revise and expand the text, to increase the number of the chapters by dividing some of the longer ones and rearranging parts of the narrative, and to introduce a number of new illustrations. At the beginning and end of each chapter, there are also introduced analyses and lists of topics, as aids to the busy teacher. With these changes it is hoped that the revised edition of the book will not merely retain the favor accorded to the original edition, but will make new friends.

January, 1912

Introduction

When Columbus in the year 1492 returned from his voyage of discovery, a keen rivalry began among the Old World nations for the possession of the New World. Expedition followed expedition; Spaniards, Portuguese, French, English, and later the Dutch and Swedes,—all began to strive with one another for the wealth and dominion of the new-found lands; and American history—our own history—begins.

But who were these Spaniards and Portuguese, these Englishmen and Frenchmen, these Dutchmen and Swedes? In the old days when the might and power of Rome ruled over the world, we hear nothing of them. Whence had they come? Were they entirely new peoples who had had no part in the old world of the Greeks and Romans? Were they the descendants of the old peoples over whom the Emperors had ruled from the city of the Seven Hills? Or did they arise by a mingling of the old and the new? Then, if they were the result of a mingling, where had the new races dwelt during the long years that Rome was spreading her empire over the known world? When and how had the mingling taken place? What, too, had become of...

"The Glory that was Greece, the grandeur that was Rome"?

Why was America not discovered and settled before? What were the customs, the ideas, the institutions which these peoples brought with them when they settled here? In short, what had been the history and what was the condition of the nations which, after 1492, began the struggle for the mastery of the New World?

To such questions it is the aim of this book to give an answer. It will try to show how the power of Rome fell before the attacks of German barbarians, and how, in the long course of the Middle Ages, new peoples, new states, a new civilization, arose on the ruins of the old.

At the beginning of the period Rome was old and worn out with misgovernment and evil living. But planted in this dying Rome there was the new and vigorous Christian Church which was to draw up into itself all that was best and strongest of the old world. The Germans were rude and uncivilized, but they were strong in mind and body, and possessed some ideas about government, women, and the family which were better than the ideas of the Romans on these subjects.

When the Germans conquered the Romans, and settled within the bounds of the Empire, it might well have seemed that the end of the world was come. Cities were plundered and destroyed; priceless works of art were dashed to pieces; and the inhabitants of many lands were slain or enslaved. For nearly a thousand years Europe did not entirely recover from the shock; and the period which immediately follows the invasions of the barbarians is so dreary and sad that historians have called it "the Dark Ages."

But what was best in the old Greek and Roman civilization did not wholly perish.

The Christian Church, too, grew steadily stronger, and sought to soften and civilize the rude Germans.

The Germans, in turn, did not lose their vigor or their good ideas.

At last from the combination of all these elements a new civilization arose,—stronger, better, and capable of higher development than the old,—and the Middle Ages were past. Then and only then could—and did—the new nations, which meanwhile had slowly been forming, set out on their careers of discovery and exploration which have made our New World possible.

So, we may say, the Middle Ages were the period when Europe became Europe, and made ready to found new Europes in America, in Australia, and in Africa. It was the growing-time for all the great harvest which has come since that time.

The Ancient Germans

We must begin our story with those new races which were to mix their blood with that of the peoples of the Roman Empire, and form the nations of Europe to-day. These were the ancient Germans, the ancestors of the peoples who now speak German, English, Dutch, and Scandinavian.

They lived then,—as part of their descendants still do,—in the lands extending from the North Sea and the Baltic on the North, to the Danube River on the South; and from the Rhine on the West, to the rivers Elbe and Oder on the East. This region is now one of the most flourishing countries in all the world, with many great cities and millions of inhabitants. At that time it had no cities at all and but few inhabitants. The people had just begun to settle down and cultivate the soil, where before they had moved from place to place to find fresh pasturage for their flocks and better hunting. The surface of the country was still almost as Nature had made it. Gloomy forests stretched for miles and miles where now there are sunny fields, and wide and treacherous marshes lay where the land now stands firm and solid.

An old German village

In this wild country, for many years, the Germans had room to live their own life. To the East were the Slavs, a people still ruder and more uncivilized than themselves. To the West were the Gauls, in what is now France. To the South were provinces of the Roman Empire, separated from them by the broad stream of the river Danube.

The Germans, the Gauls, the Slavs, and the Romans,—though they did not know it,—might all call themselves cousins; for most of the peoples of Europe are descended from one great race, called the Aryans. Long before Athens or Rome was built, before the Germans had come into this land, before any nation had begun to keep a written account of its deeds, the forefathers of these peoples dwelt together somewhere in western Asia or eastern Europe. At last, for reasons which we cannot know after so great a stretch of time, these Aryan peoples separated and moved away in different directions.

9

One branch of them entered Italy and became the ancestors of the Greeks and Romans. Another entered what is now France, and became the Gauls whom Caesar conquered. One settled in Germany, and still others settled in other lands both near and far.

In spite of the kinship between them, however, the Germans and Romans were very different in many ways. The Romans were short and dark, while the Germans were tall—very tall, they seemed to the Romans,—with fair skin, light hair, and clear blue eyes. The clothing of the Germans, unlike that of the Romans, was made chiefly from the skins of animals. Usually it did not cover the whole body, the arms and shoulders at least being left free. When the German was in a lazy mood he would sit for days by the fire, clad only in a long cloak of skins; then when he prepared to hunt or to fight, he would put on close-fitting garments and leave his cloak behind.

The houses in which the Germans lived were mere cabins or huts. Nothing was used but wood and that was not planed smooth, but was roughly hewn into boards and timbers. Sometimes a cave would be used for a dwelling, and often a house of timber would have an underground room attached to it; this was for warmth in winter and also for protection against their enemies. Sometimes in summer the people made huts of twigs woven together in much the same way that a basket is woven. Such houses were very flimsy, but they had the advantage of being easily moved from place to place. Often, too, the house sheltered not only the family, but the horses and cattle as well, all living under one roof. One can imagine that this was not a very healthful plan.

The Germans gained their living partly from hunting and partly from tilling the soil. They also depended a great deal upon their herds and flocks for meat, as well as for milk and the foods which they made from milk. The Germans paid great respect to their women, and the latter could often by their reproaches stop the men when defeated and in flight, and encourage them to do battle again. Nevertheless, the care of the cattle and the tilling of the soil, as well as the house-work, fell chiefly to the women. The men preferred to hunt or to fight; and when not doing either, would probably be found by the fire sleeping or idling away their time in games of chance. Most of the occupations of which we now see so much were not known to them. There was hardly any trading either among themselves or with other nations. Each family made its own things, and made very little more than it needed for its own use. The women spun and wove linen and other cloth, tanned leather, made soap,—which the Greeks and Romans did not know,—and a few other things. But all this was only for use in their own families. There were no trading places, and almost no commerce, except in a few things such as skins, and the amber of the Baltic Sea. One occupation, however, was considered good enough for any man to follow. This was the trade of the blacksmith. The skillful smith was highly honored, for he not only made tools to work with, but also weapons with which to hunt and to fight.

But usually the free man considered it beneath his dignity to work in any way. He was a warrior more than anything else. The Romans had reason to know that the Germans were very stubborn fighters; indeed, the Romans never did conquer Germany. The Germans were not made weak, as the Romans were, by indulging in all kinds of luxuries. They lived in the open air, they ate plain food, and they did not make their bodies tender by too much clothing. In every way their habits were more wholesome than those of the Romans; and besides this, each man had a spirit of independence that caused him to fight hard to avoid capture and slavery.

At one time, while Augustus was Emperor, three legions of the Roman army, under an officer named Varus, were entrapped and slain in the German forests. The shock of this defeat was felt so keenly at Rome that long after that the Emperor would awake at night from restless sleep, and cry out: "Varus, Varus, give me back my legions!"

After this the Romans learned to be more careful in fighting the Germans. The Romans had the advantage of better weapons with which to fight, better knowledge of how to fight, and greater wealth with which to carry on a war. So, in spite of some decided victories over the soldiers of the Empire, the Germans were obliged for many years to acknowledge Rome as the stronger; and Roman soldiers were even stationed in some parts of the German territory.

Germans going into battle

When the German army was preparing for battle, the men arranged themselves so that each line had a greater number in it and was longer than the one in front. Thus the army formed a sort of wedge, which they called the "boar's head," from its shape. Arranged in this manner the army moved forward with one grand rush, guarding their sides with large wooden shields, and hewing with their swords and thrusting with their spears. If the first rush failed to dismay the enemy and turn them in flight, there was no longer any order or plan of battle. Each man then fought for himself, until victory or defeat ended the struggle.

Among the Germans no man dared to flee from the field of battle, for cowardice was punished with death. To leave one's shield behind was the greatest of crimes, and made a man disgraced in the sight of all. Bravery was the chief of virtues, and it was this alone which could give a man the leadership of an army. The general was chosen for his valor, and he kept his position only so long as he continued to show himself brave. He must be an example to all his followers and must fight in the front ranks. A general was made by his fellow warriors, who raised him upon their shields as a sign of their choice. If he proved less worthy than they had thought, they could as easily make another general in his place. The leader and his men were constantly reminded that upon their strength and courage depended the safety and happiness of their wives and children; for their families often followed the army to battle, and witnessed the combats from rude carts or wagons, mingling their shrill cries with the din of battle.

Times of peace among these early Germans would seem to us much like war. Every man carried his weapons about with him and used them freely. Human life was held cheap, and a quarrel was often settled by the sword. There was no strong government to punish wrong and protect the weak; so men had to protect and help themselves. A man was bound to take up the quarrels, or feuds, of his family and avenge by blood a wrong done to any of his relatives. As a result there was constant fighting. Violent deeds were frequent, and their punishment was light. If a man injured another, or even committed murder, the law might be satisfied and the offender excused, by the payment of a fine to the injured man, or to his family.

Some tribes of Germans had kings, but others had not, and were ruled by persons chosen in the meetings of the people, or "folk." Even among those tribes that had kings, the power of the ruler in time of peace was not very great. The kings were not born kings, but were chosen by the consent of the people. Some few families, because they had greater wealth, or for some other reason, were looked upon with such respect that they were considered noble, and kings were chosen from among their number. Yet each man stood upon his own merits, too; and neither wealth nor birth could keep a king in power if he proved evil in rule or weak in battle. The rulers decided only the matters that were of small importance. When it came to serious matters, such as making war or changing the customs of the tribe, the "folk" assembled together decided for itself. In their assemblies they showed disapproval by loud murmurs; while to signify approval, they clashed their shields and spears together. Every free man had the right to attend the folk-meeting of his district, and also the general assembly of the whole tribe. The power of the king was less than that of the assembly, and he was subject to it; for the assembly could depose the king, as well as elect him. In times of war, however the power of the kings was much increased; for then it was necessary that one man should do the planning, and time could not be taken up with assemblies.

At the period of which we are speaking, the Germans did not believe in one God as we do, but many. The names of some of their gods are preserved in the names which we have for the days of the week. From the god Tius comes Tuesday, from Woden comes Wednesday, and from Thor comes Thursday. Tius was the god of the heavens, and was at first the chief of the gods. Songs were sung in his honor, palaces named for him, and even human beings were sacrificed to him. Woden was afterward worshiped as the god of the sky, and also of the winds. Because he controlled the winds, it was natural that he should be the special god to whom those people looked who depended upon the sea; therefore he became the protector of sailors. He was also the god of war, and the spear was his emblem. After the worship of Tius died out, Woden became the chief god of the Germans. To him also there were sacrifices of human beings. Next in importance to Woden was Thor, the god of thunder and also of the household. His emblem was a hammer. When it thundered the people said that Thor with his hammer was fighting the ice-giants; so he was regarded as the enemy of winter, and the giver of good crops.

Besides these chief gods, there were many less important ones. Among these were spirits of the forests and rivers, and the "gnomes" or dwarfs who dwelt in the earth, guarding the stores of precious metals and jewels which it contains. Long after the old religion had come to an end the descendants of the ancient Germans remembered these spirits, and stories of their tricks and good deeds were handed down from father to son. In this way the Germans kept something of the old religion in the beautiful fairy tales which we still love; and in our Christmas and Easter customs we find other traces of their old beliefs and customs.

When missionaries went among them, however, they became Christians. This shows one of the greatest qualities which they possessed. They were willing and able to learn from other peoples, and to change their customs to suit new circumstances. Other races, like the American Indians, who did not learn so readily, have declined and died away when they have been brought in contact with a higher civilization. But the Germans could learn from the Greeks and the Romans; so they grew from a rude, half-barbarous people, into great and civilized nations. Today the strongest and most progressive nations of the world are descended, wholly or in part, from these ancient Germans.

Breaking the Frontier

If you look at the map of Europe you will see two great rivers,—the Rhine and the Danube,—flowing in opposite directions across the continent, one emptying into the North Sea and the other into the Black Sea. Their mouths are thousands of miles apart; yet when you follow up the course of each, you find that they come nearer and nearer, until, at their sources, the distance between them is no greater than a good walker might cover in a day. Thus these two rivers almost form a single line across the whole of Europe. Each in its lower course is broad and deep, and makes a good boundary for the countries on its banks. The Roman armies in the old days often crossed these rivers and indeed gained victories beyond them; but they found it so hard to keep possession of what they conquered there, that in the end they decided not to try. So for many years the Rhine and the Danube rivers formed the northern boundary of the Roman Empire.

In the last chapter you have read something of the Germans who lived north and east of this boundary. Among these peoples there was one which was to take the lead in breaking through the frontier and bringing about the downfall of the great empire of Rome. This was the nation of the Goths.

In the latter part of the fourth century after Christ, the Goths dwelt along the shores of the Black Sea and just north of the lower course of the Danube River. There they had been dwelling for more than a hundred years. According to the stories which the old men had told their sons, and the sons had told their children after them, the Goths at one time had dwelt far to the North, on the shores of the Baltic. Why they left their northern home, we do not know. Perhaps it was because of a famine or a pestilence which had come upon the land; perhaps it was because of a victory or a defeat in war with their neighbors; perhaps it was because of the urging of some great leader, or because of an oracle of their gods.

At any rate, the Goths did leave their homes by the Baltic Sea, to wander southward through the forests of what is now Western Russia. After many years, they had arrived in the sunnier lands about the Danube. There they had come in contact with the Romans for the first time. For a while there had been much fighting between the two peoples; but at last the Goths had been allowed to settle down quietly in these lands, on condition that they should not cross the river Danube and enter the Roman territory. And there they had dwelt ever since, living peaceably, for the most part, alongside their Roman neighbors and learning from them many civilized ways.

The greatest thing that the Goths learned from the Romans was Christianity. Little by little they ceased worshiping Thor and Woden, and became Christians. This was chiefly due to one of their own men, named Ulfilas, who spent a number of years at Constantinople, the Roman capital of the world. There he became a Christian priest; and when he returned to his people he began to work as a missionary among them. Ulfilas had many difficulties to overcome in this work; but the chief one was that there was no Bible, or indeed any books, in the Gothic language. So Ulfilas set to work to translate the Bible from the Greek language into the Gothic. This was a hard task in itself; but it was made all the harder by the fact that before he could begin he had to invent an alphabet in which to write down the Gothic words. After the translation was made, too, he had to teach his people how to read it. In all this Ulfilas was successful; and under his wise and patient teaching the Goths rapidly became Christians. At the same time they were becoming more civilized, and their rulers were beginning to build up a great kingdom about the

Danube and the Black Sea. Suddenly, however, an event happened which was to change all their later history, and indeed the history of the world as well. This was the coming of the Huns into Europe.

The Huns were not members of the great Aryan family of nations; and indeed the Germans and the Romans thought that they were scarcely human at all. They were related to the Chinese; and their strange features and customs, and their shrill voices, were new to Europe. An old Gothic writer gives us a picture of them. "Nations whom they could never have defeated in fair fight,"

A Hun warrior

he says, "fled in horror from those frightful faces—if, indeed, I may call them faces; for they are nothing but shapeless black pieces of flesh, with little points instead of eyes. They have no hair on their cheeks or chins. Instead, the sides of their faces show deep furrowed scars; for hot irons are applied, with characteristic ferocity, to the face of every boy that is born among them, so that blood is drawn from his cheeks before he is allowed to taste his mother's milk. The men are little in size, but quick and active in their motions; and they are especially skillful in riding. They are broad-shouldered, are good at the use of the bow and arrows, have strong necks, and are always holding their heads high in their pride. To sum up, these beings under the forms of men hide the fierce natures of beasts."

The Goths were brave, but they could not stand against such men as these. The EAST-GOTHS, who dwelt about the Black Sea, were soon conquered, and for nearly a century they continued to be subject to the Huns. The WEST-GOTHS, who dwelt about the Danube, fled in terror before the countless hordes of the new-comers, and sought a refuge within the boundaries of the Roman Empire. As many as two hundred thousand fighting men, besides thousands of old men, women, and children, gathered on the north bank of the Danube, and "stretching out their hands from afar, with loud lamentations," begged the Roman officers to permit them to cross the river and settle in the Roman lands.

The Roman Emperor, after much discussion, granted their request; but only on hard conditions, for he feared to have so many of the Goths in the land. The Gothic boys, he said, must be given up to the Romans as hostages, and the men must surrender their arms. The situation of the Goths was so serious that they were forced to agree to these terms; but many of them found means to bribe the Roman officers, to let them keep their arms with them. At last the crossing began; and for many days an army of boats was kept busy ferrying the people across the stream, which at this point was more than a mile wide.

In this way the West-Goths were saved from the Huns; but they soon found that it was only to suffer many injuries at the hands of the Roman officers. The emperor had given orders that the Goths were to be fed and cared for until they could be settled on new lands; but the Roman officers stole the food intended for them, and oppressed them in other ways. Some of the Goths, indeed, fell into such distress that they sold their own children as slaves in order to get food.

This state of affairs could not last long with so war-like a people as the Goths. One day, in the midst of a banquet which the Roman governor was giving to their leader, an outcry was heard in the palace-yard, and the news came that the Goths were being attacked. At once the Gothic leader drew his sword, saying he would stop the tumult, and went out to his men.

From that time war began between the Romans and the West-Goths.

About a year after this (in the year 378 A.D.) a great battle was fought near Adrianople, a city which lies about one hundred and forty miles northwest of Constantinople. The Emperor Valens was himself at the head of the Roman army. His flatterers led him to believe that there could be no doubt of his success; so Valens rashly began the battle without waiting for the troops that were coming to assist him.

The Romans were at other disadvantages. They were hot and tired, and their horses had had no food; the men, moreover, became crowded together into a narrow space where they could neither form their lines, nor use their swords and spears with effect.

The victory of the Goths was complete. The Roman cavalry fled at the first attack; then the infantry were surrounded and cut down by thousands. More than two-thirds of the Roman army perished, and with them perished the Emperor Valens—no one knows just how.

The effects of this defeat were very disastrous for the Romans. Before this time the Goths had been doubtful of their power to defeat the Romans in the open field. Now they felt confidence in themselves, and were ready to try for new victories. And this was not the worst. After the battle of Adrianople the river Danube can no longer be considered the boundary of the Empire. The Goths had gained a footing within the frontier and could wander about at will. Other barbarian nations soon followed their example, and then still others came. As time went on, the Empire fell more and more into the hands of the barbarians.

These effects were not felt so much at first because the new Emperor, Theodosius, was an able man, and wise enough to see that the best way to treat the Goths was to make friends of them. This he did, giving them lands to till, and taking their young men into the pay of his army; so during his reign the Goths were quiet, and even helped him to fight his battles against his Roman enemies. One old chief, who had remained an enemy of the Romans, was received with kindness by Theodosius. After seeing the strength and beauty of the city of Constantinople, he said one day:

"This Emperor is doubtless a god upon earth; and whoever lifts a hand against him is guilty of his own blood."

But the wise and vigorous rule of Theodosius was a short one, and came to an end in the year 395. After that the Roman Empire was divided into an Eastern Empire, with its capital at Constantinople, and a Western Empire, with its capital at Rome. After that, too, the friendly treatment of the Goths came to an end, and a jealous and suspicious policy took its place.

Moreover, a new ruler, named Alaric, had just been chosen by the Goths. He was a fiery young prince, and was the ablest ruler that the West-Goths ever had. He had served in the Roman armies, and had there learned the Roman manner of making war. He was ambitious, too; and when he saw that the Empire was weakened by division, and by the folly of its rulers, he decided that the time had come for action.

So, as an old Gothic writer tells us, "the new King took counsel with his people and they determined to carve out new kingdoms for themselves, rather than, through idleness, to continue the subjects of others."

The Wanderings of the West-Goths

Up to this time the Goths had entered only a little way into the lands of the Empire. Now they were to begin a series of wanderings that took them into Greece, into Italy, into Gaul, and finally into the Spanish peninsula, where they settled down and established a power that lasted for nearly three hundred years.

Their leader, Alaric, was wise enough to see that the Goths could not take a city so strongly walled as Constantinople. He turned his people aside from the attack of that place, and marched them to the plunder of the rich provinces that lay to the South. There they came into lands that had long been famous in the history of the world. Their way first led them through Macedonia, whence the great Alexander had set out to conquer the East. At the pass of Thermopylae, more than eight hundred years before, a handful of heroic Greeks had held a vast army at bay for three whole days; but now their feebler descendants dared not attempt to stay the march of Alaric. The city of Athens, beautiful with marble buildings and statuary, fell into the hands of the Goths without a blow. It was forced to pay a heavy ransom, and then was left "like the bleeding and empty skin of a slaughtered victim."

From Athens Alaric led his forces by the isthmus of Corinth into the southern peninsula of Greece. City after city yielded to the conqueror without resistance. Everywhere villages were burned, cattle were driven off, precious vases, statues, gold and silver ornaments were divided among the barbarians, and multitudes of the inhabitants were slain or reduced to slavery.

Goths on the march

In all the armies of the Roman Empire, at this time, there was but one general who was a match for Alaric in daring and skill. He too was descended from the sturdy barbarians of the North. His name was Stilicho, and he was not sent by the Emperor of the West to assist the Eastern Emperor. He succeeded in hemming in the Goths, at first, in the rocky valleys of Southern Greece. But the skill and perseverance of Alaric enabled him to get his men out of the trap, while his enemies feasted and danced in enjoyment of their triumph. Then the Eastern Emperor made Alaric the ruler of one of the provinces of the Empire, and settled his people on the eastern shores of the Adriatic Sea. In this way he hoped that the Goths might again be quieted and the danger turned aside. But Alaric only used the position he had won to gather stores of food, and to manufacture shields, helmets, swords, and spears for his men, in preparation for new adventures.

When all was ready, Alaric again set out, taking with him the entire nation of the West-Goths—men, women, and children—together with all their property and the booty which they had won in Greece. Now their march was to the rich and beautiful lands of Italy, where Alaric hoped to capture Rome itself, and secure the treasures which the Romans had gathered from the ends of the earth.

But the time had not yet come for this. Stilicho was again in arms before him in the broad plains of the river Po. From Gaul, from the provinces of the Rhine, from far-off Britain, troops were hurried to the protection of Italy. On every side the Goths were threatened. Their long-haired chiefs, scarred with honorable wounds, began to hesitate; but their fiery young King cried out that he was resolved "to find in Italy either a kingdom or a grave!"

At last while the Goths were piously celebrating the festival of Easter, the army of Stilicho suddenly attacked them. The Goths fought stubbornly; but after a long and bloody battle Alaric was obliged to lead his men from the field, leaving behind them the slaves and the booty which they had won.

Even then Alaric did not at once give up his plan of forcing his way to Rome. But his men were discouraged; hunger and disease attacked them; their allies deserted them; and at last the young King was obliged to lead his men back to the province on the Adriatic.

For six years Alaric now awaited his time; while Stilicho, meanwhile, beat back other invaders who sought to come into Italy. But the Western Emperor was foolish, and thought the danger was past. He listened to the enemies of Stilicho, and quarreled with him; and at last he had him put to death. At once Alaric planned a new invasion. Barbarian warriors from all lands, attracted by his fame, flocked to his standard. The friends of Stilicho, also, came to his aid. The new generals in Italy proved to be worthless; and the foolish Emperor shut himself up in fear in his palace in the northern part of the peninsula. Alaric meanwhile did not tarry. On and on he pressed, over the Alps, past the plains of the Po, past the palace of the Emperor, on to the "eternal city" of Rome itself.

In the old days, the Romans had been able to conquer Italy and the civilized world, because they were a brave, sturdy people, with a genius for war and for government. But long centuries of unchecked rule had greatly weakened them. Now they led evil and unhealthy lives. They neither worked for themselves, nor fought in their country's cause. Instead, they spent their days in marble baths, at the gladiatorial fights and wild beast shows of the theaters, and in lounging about the Forum.

In the old days Hannibal had thundered at the gates of Rome in vain; but it was not to be so now with Alaric. Three times in three successive years he advanced to the siege of the city. The first time he blockaded it till the people cried out in their hunger and were forced to eat loathsome food. Still no help came from the Emperor, and when they tried to overawe Alaric with the boast of the numbers of their city, he only replied: "The thicker the hay the easier it is mowed."

When asked what terms he would give them, Alaric demanded as ransom all their gold, silver, and precious goods, together with their slaves who were of barbarian blood. In dismay they asked: "And what then will you leave to us?" "Your lives," he grimly replied.

Alaric, however, was not so hard as his word. On payment of a less ransom than he had at first demanded, he consented to retire. But when the foolish Emperor, secure in his palace in Northern Italy, refused to make peace, Alaric advanced once more upon the doomed city, and again it submitted. This time Alaric set up a mock-Emperor of his own to rule. But in a few months he grew tired of him, and overturned him with as little thought as he had shown in setting him up. As a great historian tells us of this Emperor, he was in turn "promoted, degraded, insulted, restored, again degraded, and again insulted, and finally abandoned to his fate."

In the year 410 A.D., Alaric advanced a third time upon the city. This time the gates of Rome were opened by slaves who hoped to gain freedom through the city's fall. For the first time since the burning of Rome by the Gauls, eight hundred years before, the Romans now saw a foreign foe within their gates—slaying, destroying, plundering, committing endless outrages upon the people and their property. To the Romans it seemed that the end of the world was surely at hand.

At the end of the sixth day Alaric and his Goths came forth from the city, carrying their booty and their captives with them. They now marched into the south of Italy, destroying all who resisted and plundering what took their fancy. In this way they came into the southernmost part. There they began busily preparing to cross over into Sicily, to plunder that fertile province.

West-Gothic tower

But this was not to be. In the midst of the preparations, their leader Alaric—"Alaric the Bold," as they loved to call him—suddenly sickened. Soon he grew worse; and after an illness of only a few days, he died, leaving the Goths weakened by the loss of the greatest king they were ever to know.

Alaric's life had been one of the strangest in history; and his burial was equally strange. His followers wished to lay him where no enemy might disturb his grave. To this end they compelled their captives to dig a new channel for a little river near by, and turn aside its waters. Then, in the old bed of the stream, they buried their beloved leader, clad in his richest armor, and mounted upon his favorite war horse. When all was finished, the stream was turned back into its old channel, and the captives were slain, in order that they might not reveal the place of the burial. And there, to this day, rest the bones of Alaric, the West-Gothic King.

Of the West-Goths after the death of Alaric, we need say very little. The foolish Emperor of the West remained foolish to the end; but his advisers now saw that something must be done to get rid of the barbarians. The new leader of the Goths, too, was a wise and moderate man. He saw that his people, though they could fight well, and overturn a state, were not yet ready to take the government of Rome for themselves.

"I wish," he said, "not to destroy, but to restore and maintain the prosperity of the Roman Empire."

Other barbarians had meanwhile pressed into the Empire; so it was agreed that the Goths should march into Gaul and Spain, drive out the barbarians who had pushed in there, and rule the land in the name of the Emperor of the

West. This they did; and there they established a power which became strong and prosperous, and lasted until new barbarians from the North, and the Moors from Africa, pressed in upon them, and brought, at the same time, their kingdom and their history to an end.

Fall of the Western Empire

While the West-Goths were winning lands and booty within the Empire, the other Germans could not long remain idle. They saw that the legions had been recalled from the frontiers in order to guard Italy. They saw their own people suffering from hunger and want. Behind them, too, they felt the pressure of other nations, driving them from their pastures and hunting grounds.

So the news of Rome's weakness and Alaric's victories filled other peoples with eagerness to try their fortunes in the Southern lands. Before the Wast-Goths had settled down in Spain, other tribes had begun to stream across the borders of the Empire. Soon the stream became a flood, and the flood a deluge. All Germany seemed stirred up and hurled against the Empire. Wave after wave swept southward. Horde after horde appeared within the limits of the Empire, seeking lands and goods.

For two hundred years this went on. Armies and nations went wandering up and down, burning, robbing, slaying, and making captives. It was a time of confusion, suffering, and change; when the "uncouth Goth," the "horrid Hun," and wild-eyed peoples of many names, struggled for the lands of Rome. They sought only their own gain and advantage, and it seemed that everything was being overturned and nothing built up to take the place of what was destroyed.

But this was only in seeming. Unknowingly, these nations were laying the foundations of a new civilization and a new world. For out of this mixing of peoples and institutions, this blending of civilizations, arose the nations, the states, the institutions, of the world of to-day.

In following the history of the West-Goths we have seen that some of these peoples had preceded the Goths into Spain. These were a race called the VANDALS. They too were of German blood. At one time they had dwelt on the shores of the Baltic Sea, near the mouth of the river Elbe. From there they had wandered southward and westward, struggling with other barbarian tribes and with the remaining troops of Rome's imperial army. After many hard-fought contests they had crossed the river Rhine. They had then struggled through Gaul, and at last had reached Spain. Now they were to be driven from that land, too, by the arrival of the West-Goths.

Just at this time the governor of the Roman province of Africa rebelled against the Emperor's government. To get assistance against the Romans, he invited the Vandals to come to Africa, promising them lands and booty. The Vandals needed no second invitation. The Strait of Gibraltar, which separates the shores of Spain from Africa, is only fifteen miles wide; but when once the Vandals were across that strait, they were never to be driven back again.

Court of the Huns

Twenty-five thousand warriors, together with their women, children, and the old men, came at the call of the rebellious governor. There they set up a kingdom of their own on Roman soil. A cruel, greedy people they were, but able. From their capital,—the old city of Carthage,—their pirate ships rowed up and down the Mediterranean, stopping now at this place and now at that, wherever they saw a chance for plunder. Their King was the most crafty, the most treacherous, the most merciless of the barbarian kings.

"Whither shall we sail?" asked his pilot one day, as the King and his men set out. "Guide us," said the King, "wherever there is a people with whom God is angry."

The most famous of the Vandal raids was the one which they made on the city of Rome, forty-five years after it had been plundered by Alaric. The rulers of the Romans were as worthless now as they had been at the earlier day. Again, too, it was at the invitation of a Roman that the Vandals invaded Roman territory. No defense of the city was attempted; but Leo, the holy bishop of Rome, went out with his priests, and tried to soften the fierceness of the barbarian King. For fourteen days the city remained in the hands of the Vandals; and it was plundered to their hearts' content. Besides much rich booty which they carried off, many works of art were broken and destroyed. Because of such destruction as this, the name "Vandal" is still given to anyone who destroys beautiful or useful things recklessly, or solely for the sake of destroying them.

Another of the restless German peoples were the BURGUNDIANS. They, too, had once dwelt in the North of German, and had crossed the river Rhine in company with the Vandals. Gradually they had then spread southward into Gaul; and the result was the founding of a kingdom of the Burgundians in the valley of the Rhone River. From

Coin of Odoacer

that day to this the name Burgundy,—as kingdom, dukedom, county, province,—has remained a famous one in the geography of Europe. But this people was never able to grow into a powerful and independent nation.

While the Germans were finding new homes in Roman territory, the restless Huns were ever pressing in from the rear, driving them on and taking their lands as they left. At the time when the Vandals were establishing their kingdom in Africa, and the Saxons were just beginning to come into Britain, a great King arose among the Huns. His name was Attila. Though he was a great warrior and ruler, he was far from being a handsome man. He had a large head, a flat nose, a few hairs in the place of a beard, broad shoulders, and a short square body.

The chief god of the Huns was a god of war. As they did not know how to make statues or images of him, they represented him by a sword or dagger. One day a shepherd found an old sword sticking out of the ground, and brought it to Attila. This, the King said, was a sign that the whole earth should be ruled over by him.

Whether he believed in this sign himself or not, Attila used his own sword so successfully that he formed the scattered tribes of the Huns into a great nation. By wars and treaties he succeeded in establishing a vast empire, including all the peoples from the river Volga to the river Rhine. The lands of the Eastern Empire, too, were wasted by him, even up to the walls of Constantinople. The Empire was forced to pay him tribute; and an Emperor's sister sent him her ring, and begged him to rescue her from the convent in which her brother had confined her.

In the year 451 A.D., Attila gathered up his wild horsemen, and set out from his wooden capital in the valley of the Danube. Southward and westward they swept to conquer and destroy. It is said that Attila called himself the "Scourge of God." At any rate his victims knew that ruin and destruction followed in his track; and where he had passed, they said, not a blade of grass was left growing. On and on the Huns passed, through Germany, as far as Western Gaul; and men expected that all Europe would fall under the rule of this fierce people.

This, however, did not come to pass. Near the city of Chalons, in Eastern France, a great battle was fought, in which Romans and Goths fought side by side against the common foe, and all the peoples of Europe seemed engaged in one battle. Rivers of blood, it was said, flowed through the field, and whoever drank of their waters perished. At the close of the first day, the victory was still uncertain. On the next day Attila refused to renew the battle; and when the Romans and Goths drew near his camp, they found it silent and empty. The Huns had slipped away in the night, and returned to their homes on the Danube.

Many legends came to cluster about this battle. In later ages men told how, each year on the night of the battle, the spirits of Goths and Huns arose from their graves, and fought the battle over again in the clouds of the upper air.

The next year Attila came again, with a mighty army, into the Roman lands. This time he turned his attention to Italy. A city lying at the head of the Adriatic was destroyed; and its people then founded Venice on the isles of the sea, that they might thenceforth be free from such attacks. Perhaps Attila might have pressed on to Rome and taken it, too, as Alaric had done, and as the Vandals were to do three years later. But strange misgivings fell upon him. Leo, the holy bishop of Rome, appeared in his court and warned him off. Attila, therefore, retreated, and left Rome untouched. Within two years afterward he died; and then his great empire dropped to pieces, and his people fell to fighting once more among themselves. In this way Christian Europe was delivered from one of the greatest dangers that ever threatened it.

Gaul, Spain, Africa, and Britain, had now been lost by the Romans; but amid all these troubles, the imperial government, both in the East and in the West, still went on. In the West the power had fallen more and more into the hands of chiefs of the Roman army. These men were often barbarians by blood, and did not care to be emperors themselves. Instead, however, they set up and pulled down emperors at will, as Alaric had once done.

In the year 476 A.D.—just thirteen hundred years before the signing of our Declaration of Independence,—the Emperor who was then ruling in the West was a boy of tender years, named Romulus Augustus. He bore the names of the first of the kings of Rome, and of the first of the emperors; but he was to be the last of either. A new leader had now arisen in the army,—a gigantic German, named Odoacer. When Odoacer was about to come into Italy to enter the Roman army, a holy hermit had said to him: "Follow out your plan, and go. There you will soon be able to throw away the coarse garment of skins which you now wear, and will become wealthy and powerful."

He had followed this advice, and had risen to be the commander of the Roman army. The old leader, who had put Romulus Augustulus on the throne, was now slain by Odoacer, and the boy was then quietly put aside.

Odoacer thus made himself ruler of Italy; but he neither took the name of Emperor himself, nor gave it to any one else. He sent messengers instead to the Emperor of the East, at Constantinople, and laid at his feet the crown and purple robe. He said, in actions, if not in words: "One Emperor is enough for both East and West. I will rule Italy in your name and as your agent."

This is sometimes called the fall of the Western Empire; and so it was. Yet there was not so very much change at first. Odoacer ruled in Italy in much the same way as the Emperors had done, except that his rule was better and stronger.

East-Goths and Lombards

After sixteen years Odoacer was overthrown, and a new ruler arose in his place. This was Theodoric, the King of the EAST-GOTHS. From the days of the battle of Adrianople to the death of Attila, this people had been subject to the Huns. At the battle of Chalons they had fought on the side of the Huns, and against their kinsmen, the West-Goths. Now, however, they were free; and a great leader had arisen among them in the person of Theodoric, the descendant of a long line of Gothic kings.

When Theodoric was a young boy, he had been sent as a hostage to Constantinople, where he had lived for ten years. There he had learned to like the cultured manners of the Romans, but he had not forgotten how to fight. When he had returned home, a handsome lad of seventeen, he had gathered together an army, and without guidance from his father, had captured an important city. This act showed his ability; and when his father died he was acknowledged as the King of his people. He was a man of great strength and courage; he was also wise and anxious for his people to improve. For some years his people had been wandering up and down in the Eastern Empire; but they were unable to master that land because of Constantinople's massive walls. So, with the consent of the Emperor, Theodoric now decided to lead his East-Goths into Italy, drive Odoacer from the land, and settle his people there.

The Goths set out over the Eastern Alps, two hundred thousand strong. With them went their wives and children, their slaves and cattle, and behind came twenty thousand lumbering ox carts laden with their goods. But Odoacer proved a stubborn fighter. Several hard battles had to be fought, and a siege three years long had to be laid to his capital before he was beaten. Then Theodoric, for almost the first and last time in his life, did a mean and treacherous act. His conquered enemy was invited to a friendly banquet; and there he was put to death with his own sword.

In this way Theodoric completed the conquest that made him master of the whole of Italy, together with a large territory to the North and East of the Adriatic Sea.

For thirty-three years after that, Theodoric ruled over the kingdom of the East-Goths, as a wise and able king. Equal justice was granted to all, whether they were Goths or Italians; and Theodoric sought in every way to lead his people into a settled and civilized life. The old roads, aqueducts, and public buildings were repaired; and new works in many places were erected.

Tomb of Theodoric

Theodoric was not only a great warrior and statesman; he was also a man of deep and wide thought. If any man and any people were suited to build up a new kingdom out of the ruins of the Empire, and end the long period of disorder and confusion which we call the Dark Ages, it would seem that it was Theodoric, and his East-Goths. But no sooner was Theodoric dead, than his kingdom began to fall to pieces.

The Eastern Empire had now passed into the hands of an able Emperor, who is renowned as a conqueror, a builder, and a law-giver. His name was JUSTINIAN; and he was served by men as great as himself. Under their skillful attacks, much of the lands which had been lost were now won back. The Vandal kingdom in Africa was overturned; the islands of Sicily, Corsica, and Sardinia were recovered; and at last, after years of hard fighting, the East-Goths too were conquered. The last remnant of that race then wandered north of the Alps, and disappeared from history.

It was only for a little while, however, that the Eastern Emperor was able once more to rule all Italy. Within thirteen years a new Germanic people appeared on the scene,—the last to find a settlement within the Empire. These were the LOMBARDS, or "Langobards," as they were called from their long beards. Ten generations before, according to their legends, a wise queen had led their race across the Baltic Sea, from what is now Sweden, to Germany. Since then they had gradually

Ivory Comb of a Lombard queen

worked their way south, until now they were on the borders of Italy. The northern parts of the peninsula at this time were almost uninhabited, as a result of years of war and pestilence. The resistance to the Lombards, therefore, was very weak; and the whole valley of the river Po—thenceforth to this day called "Lombard"—passed into their hands almost at a blow.

These Lombards were a rude people and but little civilized, when they first entered Italy. It was not until some time after they had settled there, that they even became Christians. A wild story is told of the King who led them into Italy. He had slain with his own hand the King of another German folk, and from his enemy's skull he had made a drinking cup, mounted in gold. His wife was the daughter of the King he had slain. Some time after, as he sat long at the table in his capital, he grew boisterous; and sending for the cup, he forced his Queen to drink from it bidding her "drink joyfully with her father." At this the Queen's heart was filled with grief and anger, and she plotted how she might revenge her father upon her husband. So, while the King slept one night, she caused an armed man to creep into the room and slay him. In this way she secured her revenge; but she, and all who had helped her, came to evil ends,—for, as an old writer says, "the hand of Heaven was upon them for doing so foul a deed."

The Lombards were not so strongly united as most of the Germans, nor was their form of government so highly developed. Many independent bands of Lombards settled districts in Central and Southern Italy, under the rule of their own leaders, or "dukes." In this way the peninsula was cut up into many governments. The northern part was under the Lombard King; a number of petty dukes each ruled over his own district; and the remainder, including the city of Rome, was ruled by the officers of the Eastern Emperor.

The kingdom of the Lombards lasted for about two hundred years. Then it, too, was overturned, and the land was conquered by a new German people, the greatest of them all and the only one, with the exception of the English, that was to establish a lasting kingdom. These were the FRANKS, who settled in Gaul, and founded France. But before we trace their history we must first turn aside and see how the Christian Church was gaining in strength and power in this dark period of warfare and confusion.

Growth of the Christian Church

In another book you may have read of the trials which the early Christians had to endure under the Roman rule;—of how they were looked upon with scorn and suspicion; how they were persecuted; how they were forced to meet in secret caves called catacombs, where they worshiped, and buried their dead; and how at last, after many martyrs had shed their blood in witness to their faith, the Emperor Constantine allowed them to worship freely, and even himself became a Christian. After this, Christianity had spread rapidly in the Roman Empire; so that by the time the German tribes began to pour across the borders, almost all of the people who were ruled by the Emperor had adopted the Christian religion, and the old Roman worship of Jupiter, Mars, and Minerva was fast becoming a thing of the past.

Bishop, holding the crozier, on throne

When Christianity had become the religion of many people, it was necessary for the Church to have some form of organization; and such an organization speedily began to grow. First we find some of the Christians set aside to act as priests, and have charge of the services in the church. We find next among the priests in each city one who comes to be styled the "overseeing priest" or bishop, whose duty it was to look after the affairs of the churches in his district. Gradually, too, the bishops in the more important cities come to have certain powers over the bishops of the smaller cities about them; these were then called "archbishops." And finally, there came to be one out of the many hundred bishops of the Church who was looked up to more than any other person, and whose advice was sought in all important Church questions. This was because he had charge of the church in Rome, the most important city of the Empire, and because he was believed to be the successor of St. Peter, the chief of the Apostles. The name "Pope," which means father, was given to him; and it was his duty to watch over all the affairs of the Church on earth, as a father watches over the affairs of his family.

Of course, all this organization did not spring up at once, ready made. Great things grow slowly; and it was only slowly that this organization grew. Sometimes disputes arose as to the amount of power the priests should have over the "laymen," as those who were priests were called; and sometimes there were disputes among the "clergy" or churchmen, themselves. Sometimes these disputes were about power, and lands, and things of that sort; for now the Church had become wealthy and powerful, through gifts made to it by rulers and pious laymen. More often the questions to be settled had to do with the belief of the Church,—that is, with the exact meaning of the teachings of Christ and the Apostles, as they are recorded in the Bible and in the writings of the early Christian teachers. Many of the questions which were discussed seem strange to us; but men were very much in earnest about them then. And at times, when a hard question arose concerning the belief of the Church, men would travel hundreds of miles to the great Church Councils or meetings where the matter was to be decided, and undergo hardships and sufferings without number, to see that the question was decided as they thought was right.

One of the questions which caused most trouble was brought forward by an Egyptian priest named Arius. He claimed that Christ the Son was not equal in power and glory to God the Father. Another Egyptian priest named Athanasius thought this was a wrong belief, or "heresy"; so he combated the belief of Arius in every way that he could. Soon the whole Christian world rang with the controversy. To settle the dispute the first great Council of the Church was called by the Emperor Constantine in the year 325 A.D.It met at Nicaea, a city in Asia Minor. There "Arianism" was condemned, and the teaching of Athanasius was declared to be the true belief of the Church. But this did not end the struggle. The followers of Arius would not give up, and for a while they were stronger than their opponents. Five times Athanasius was driven from his position of archbishop in Egypt, and for twenty years he was forced to live an exile from his native land But he never faltered, and never ceased to write, preach, and argue for the belief which the Council had declared to be the true one. Even after Arius and Athanasius were both dead, the quarrel still went on. Indeed, it was nearly two hundred years before the last of the "Arians" gave up their view of the matter; but in the end the teachings of Athanasius became the belief of the whole Church.

One consequence of this dispute about Arianism was that the churches in the East and West began to drift apart. The Western churches followed the lead of the bishop of Rome and supported Athanasius in the struggle, while the Eastern churches for a time supported Arius. Even after Arianism had been given up, a quarrel still existed concerning the relation of the Holy Ghost to the Father and Son. As time went on, still other disputes arose between the East and West. The Roman clergy shaved their faces and were not permitted to marry, while the Greek clergy let their beards grow, and married and had children. Moreover Rome and Constantinople could not agree as to whether leavened or unleavened bread should be used in the Lord's Supper. Still less could the great bishop of Constantinople, where the Emperor held his court, admit that the power of the bishop of Rome was above his own. Each side looked with contempt and distrust upon the other; for the one were Greeks and the other Latins, and the differences of race and language made it difficult for them to understand one another.

Gradually the breach grew wider and wider. At last, after many, many years of ill feeling, the two churches broke off all relations. After that there was always a Greek Catholic Church (which exists to this day) as well as a Roman one; and the power of the Pope was acknowledged only by the churches in the Western or Latin half of the world.

The Church, of course, was as much changed by the conquests of the Germans as was the rest of the Roman world. The barbarians who settled in the lands of the Empire had already become Christians, for the most part, before the conquest, but they

A monk

were still ignorant barbarians. Worst of all, the views which they had been taught at first were those held by the Arians; and this made them more feared and hated by the Roman Christians. Among the citizens of the Empire, as well as among the barbarians, there was also much wickedness, oppression, and unfair dealing.

"The world is full of confusion," wrote one holy man. "No one trusts any one; each man is afraid of his neighbor. Many are the fleeces beneath which are concealed innumerable wolves, so that one might live more safely among enemies than among those who appear to be friends."

The result of this was that man began to turn from the world to God. Many went out into the deserts of Egypt, and other waste and solitary places, and became hermits. There they lived, clothed in rags or the skins of wild beasts, and eating the coarsest food, in order that they might escape from the temptations of the world. The more they punished their bodies, the more they thought it helped their souls; so all sorts of strange deeds were performed by them. Perhaps the strangest case of all was that of a man named Simeon, who was called "Stylites," from the way in which he lived. For thirty years,—day and night, summer and winter,—he dwelt on the top of a high pillar, so narrow that there was barely room for him to lie down. There for hours at a time he would stand praying, with his arms stretched out in the form of a cross; or else he would pass hours bowing his wasted body rapidly from his forehead to his feet, until at times the people who stood by counted a thousand bows without a single stop.

Such things as these happened more frequently in the Eastern than they did in the Western Church. In the West, men were more practical, and when they wished to flee from the world, they went into waste places and founded "monasteries," where the "monks," as they were called, dwelt together under the rule of an abbot.

In the West, too, the power of the bishop of Rome became much greater than that possessed in the East by the bishop of Constantinople. It was because the Pope was already the leading man in Rome that Leo went out to meet the Huns and the Vandals, and tried to save Rome from them. About one hundred and forty years later, Pope Gregory the Great occupied even a higher position. He not only had charge of the churches near Rome, and was looked up to by the churches of Gaul, Spain and Africa more than Leo had been; but he also ruled the land about Rome much as an emperor or king ruled his kingdom.

Gregory was born of a noble and wealthy Roman family. When he inherited his fortune he gave it all to found seven monasteries, and he himself became a monk in one of these. There he lived a severe and studious life. At length, against his own wishes, he was chosen by the clergy and people to be Pope. This was in the very midst of the Dark Ages. The Lombards had just come into Italy, and everything was in confusion. Everywhere cities were ruined, churches burned, and monasteries destroyed. Farms were laid waste and left uncultivated; and wild beasts roamed over the deserted fields. For twenty-seven years, Gregory wrote, Rome had been in terror of the sword of the Lombards. "What is happening in other countries," he said, "we know not; but in this the end of the world seems not only to be approaching, but to have actually begun." The rulers that the Eastern Emperors set up in Italy, after it had been recovered from the East-Goths, either could not or would not help. And to make matters worse, famine and sickness came, and the people died by hundreds.

So Gregory was obliged to act not only as the bishop of Rome, but as its ruler also. He caused processions to march about the city, and prayers to be said, to stop the sickness. He caused grain to be brought and given to the people, so that they might no longer die of famine. He also defended the city against the Lombards, until a peace could be made. In this way a beginning was made of the rule of the Pope over Rome, which did not come to an end until the year 1871.

Gregory was not only bishop of Rome, and ruler of the city. He was also the head of the whole Western Church, and was constantly busy with its affairs.

Before he was chosen Pope, Gregory was passing through the market-place at Rome, one day, and came to the spot where slaves—white slaves—were sold. There he saw some beautiful, fair-haired boys.

"From what country do these boys come?" he asked.

"From the island of Britain," was the answer.

"Are they Christians?"

"No," he was told; "they are still pagans."

"Alas!" exclaimed Gregory, "that the Prince of Darkness should have power over forms of such loveliness."

Then he asked of what nation they were.

"They are Angles," replied their owner.

"Truly," said Gregory, "they seem like angels, not Angles. From what province of Britain are they?"

"From Deira," said the man naming a kingdom in the northern part of the island.

"Then," said Gregory, making a pun in the Latin, "they must be rescued *de ira* [from the wrath of God]. And what is the name of their king?"

"Aella," was the answer.

"Yea," said Gregory, as he turned to go, "Alleluia must be sung in the land of Aella."

At first Gregory planned to go himself as missionary to convert the Angles and Saxons. In this he was disappointed; but when he became Pope he sent a monk named Augustine as leader of a band of missionaries. By their preaching, Christianity was introduced into the English kingdoms, and the English were gradually won from the old German worship of Woden and Thor.

Gregory also had an important part in winning the West-Goths and Lombards from Arianism to the true faith. In all that he did Gregory's action seemed so wise and good that men said he was counselled by the Holy Spirit; and in the pictures of him the Holy Spirit is always represented, in the form of a dove, hovering about his head.

Gregory has been called the real father of the Papacy of the Middle Ages. This is no small praise, for the Papacy, in those dark ages, was of great service to Christendom. In later ages, popes sometimes became corrupt; and at last the Reformation came, in which many nations of the West threw off their obedience. But in the dark days of the Middle Ages, all the Western nations looked up to the Pope as the head of the Church on earth, and the influence of the popes was for good. There was very little order, union, and love for right and justice in the Middle Ages, as it was; but no one can imagine how much greater would have been the confusion, the lawlessness, and the disorder without the restraining influence of the Papacy.

Rise of the Franks

The West-Goths, the Burgundians, the Vandals, the East-Goths, and the Lombards, all helped in their own way to make Europe what it is to-day; yet none of them succeeded in founding a power that was to last as a separate state. Their work was largely to break down the rule of the Western Empire. The building up of a new state to take its place was to be the work of another people, the FRANKS.

The Franks were the earliest of all the Germanic invaders to fix themselves in the Roman province of Gaul, but they were the last to establish a power of their own in that land.

Gaul, in the five hundred years that had passed since its conquest by Julius Caesar, had become more Roman even than Italy itself. In its long rule by foreigners, however, it had decayed in strength. The spirit of patriotism had died out; the people in the latter days of the Empire had been ground down by oppressive taxation; so it no more than the other provinces was able to offer resistance to the barbarians.

A hundred years before the West-Goths crossed the Danube, bands of the Franks had been allowed to cross the Rhine, from their homes on the right bank of that river, and to establish themselves as the allies or subjects of Rome on the western bank. There they had dwelt, gaining in numbers and in power, until news came of the deeds of Alaric. When the Vandals, Burgundians, and other Germanic tribes sought to cross the Rhine, the Franks on the left bank resisted them, but their resistance had been overcome.

Franks crossing the Rhine

Then the Franks also set out to build up a power of their own within the Roman territory. Gradually they occupied what is now northern France, together with Belgium and Holland. When the Huns swept into Gaul, the Franks had fought against them, side by side with the Romans and West-Goths. And when Attila was defeated and had retired, the Franks were allowed to take possession of certain cities in the valley of the Rhine which the Huns had won from the Romans.

So, by the time that Odoacer overthrew the last of the Roman Emperors of the West, the Franks had succeeded in getting a good footing in the Empire. But they were yet far from strong as a people. They were still heathen, and they had not yet learned, like the Goths, to wear armor or fight on horseback. They still went to war half-naked, armed only with a barbed javelin, a sword, and an ax or tomahawk. They were not united, but were divided into a large number of small tribes, each ruled over by its own petty king.

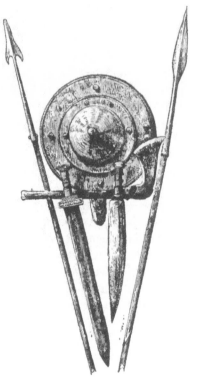

Arms of Franks

Besides all this, they had many rivals, even in Gaul itself. In the southern part of that land, reaching across the Pyrenees and taking in nearly the whole of Spain was the kingdom of the West-Goths. In the southeastern part was the kingdom of the Burgundians. In the central part, the region that included the river Seine, a Roman officer named Syagrius still ruled, though the last of the Emperors of the West had fallen. And to the East of Gaul, were tribes who still remained on German soil—the Thuringians, some tribes of the Saxons, and the Allemanians.

It was mainly due to one man that the Frankish power was not overcome, but instead was able to overcome all its enemies. This man was Clovis, the King of one of the little bands of the Franks. Five years after the fall of Rome, he had succeeded his father as King of his tribe. Though he was only sixteen years of age at that time, he soon proved himself to be one of the ablest, but alas, one of the craftiest and cruelest leaders of this crafty and cruel people. In the thirty years that he ruled, he united all the Franks under his own rule; he greatly improved the arms and organization of the army; he extended their territory to the South, East, and West; and he caused his people to be baptized as Christians.

One of the first deeds of Clovis was to make war on Syagrius, the Roman ruler. In this war the Franks were completely successful. Syagrius was defeated, and put to death; and the district over which he ruled became subject to Clovis. A story is told of this war which shows the rude and independent spirit of the Franks. When the booty was being divided by lot after the battle, Clovis wished to obtain a beautiful vase that had been taken from one of the churches, that he might return it to the priests. But one of his Franks cried out:

"Thou shalt have only what the lot gives thee!" And saying this he broke the vase with his battle-ax.

Clovis could do nothing then to resent this insult. But the next year he detected this soldier in a fault, and slew him in the presence of the army, saying:

"It shall be done to thee as thou didst to the vase!"

After the overthrow of Syagrius, Clovis turned to the conquest of other neighbors. One by one he set to work to get rid of the other kings of the Franks. Some he conquered by force; others he overcame by treachery. He persuaded the son of one king to kill his father; then he had the son put to death for the crime, and persuaded the people to take him as their king. Another king and his son were slain be-cause they had failed to help Clovis in his wars; and

A Frankish chief

he took their kingdom also. A third king was slain by Clovis's own hand, after he had been betrayed into his power. Still others of his rivals and relatives were got rid of in the same way. Then, when all were gone, he assembled the people and said:

"Alas! I have now no relatives to lend me aid in time of need."

But he did this, as an old writer says, not because he was made sad by their death, but craftily, that he might discover whether there remained any one else to kill.

In this way Clovis made himself sole King of the Franks. Already he had begun to extend his rule over other branches of the German people. The Al-lemanians, who dwelt to the eastward of the Franks, were beaten in a war which lasted several years, and were forced to take the King of the Franks as their overlord. After this the Franks began to settle in the valley of the river Main, where the Allemanians had dwelt; and in course of time this district came to be called Franconia, from their name.

Several wars too were waged between Clovis and the Burgundians; and here also the power of the Franks was increased. Most important of all were the conquests made from the West-Goths, who held Southern Gaul and Spain. Again and again Clovis led his Franks against this people. At one time Theodoric, the king of the East-Goths came to their aid and defeated Clovis with terrible slaughter. But in the end the Franks were victorious, and most of Southern Gaul was added to the Frankish territory.

Thus Clovis won for the Franks a kingdom which reached from the River Rhine on the North and East, almost to the Pyrenees Mountains on the South. To all this land, which before had borne the name Gaul, the name "Francia" was gradually applied, from the race that conquered it; and under the name of France it is still one of the most powerful states of Europe.

When Clovis first became King, the Franks worshiped the old gods, Woden and Thor. Before he died, however, he and most of his people had been baptized and become Christians. His conversion came about in this way. While he was fighting against the Allemanians, he saw his Franks one day driven from the field by the enemy. He prayed to the old gods to turn the defeat into victory; but still his troops gave way. Then he bethought him that his wife Clotilda had long been urging him to give up his old gods and become a Christian. He determined now to try the God of his wife; so he cried out:

"O Christ Jesus, I beseech thee for aid! If thou wilt grant me victory over these enemies, I will believe in thee and be baptized in thy name!"

With this he renewed the battle, and at last won a great victory. As a result, Clovis became a Christian, and more than half of his warriors decided to follow his example. When the news was brought to the priests, they were filled with joy, and at once preparations were made for the baptism. Painted awnings were hung over the streets. The churches were draped in white, and clouds of sweet smelling smoke arose from the censers in which incense was burning. The King was baptized first, and as he approached the basin the bishop cried out:

"Bow thy head, O King, and adore that which thou hast burned, and burn that which thou hast adored!"

After this, Clovis was, in name, a Christian; but his conversion was only half a conversion. He changed his beliefs, but not his conduct. When the story was told him of the way Jesus suffered death on the cross, he grasped his battle-ax fiercely and exclaimed:

"If I had been there with my Franks I would have revenged his wrongs!"

So, in spite of his conversion, Clovis remained a rude warrior, a cruel and unscrupulous ruler. Nevertheless, his conversion was of very great importance. The Goths, Vandals, and Burgundians, had all been Christians at the time they invaded the Empire, but their Christianity was not of the kind the Romans of the West accepted. They were Arian Christians, and, as we have seen, there was great hatred between the Arians and the Roman or Athanasian Christians. In Africa, Spain, and Italy, therefore, the people hated their Arian masters. But it was different with the Franks. Because they believed as the Roman Christians did, their Roman subjects in Gaul accepted and supported their rule, and the Pope showed himself friendly to them.

This is one of the two chief reasons why the Frankish power was permanent. The other reason was that the Franks did not wholly leave their old home, as the other Germans did when they set out on their conquest. The Franks kept what they already had, while adding to it the neighboring lands which they had conquered. So their increase in power was a growth, as well as a conquest; and this made it more lasting.

When the barbarians conquered portions of the Roman Empire they did not kill or drive out the people who already lived there. Usually they contented themselves with taking some of the lands for themselves, and making the people pay to them the taxes which they had before paid to the Roman emperors. So it was with the Franks. The people of Gaul were allowed to remain, and to keep most of their lands; but the Franks, although they were not nearly so numerous as the Romans, ruled over the state. The old inhabitants were highly civilized while the Franks were just taking the first steps in civilization.

"We make fun of them," wrote one of these Romans, "we despise them,—but we fear them also."

As the years went by, the differences between the conquerors and the conquered became less. The Romans found that times were changed and they had to adopt the habits of the Franks in some respects. The Franks had already adopted the religion of their subjects; they began also to adopt their language and some of their customs. In this way, the two peoples at last became as one; but it was not until long after the time of Clovis that this end was fully reached.

Descendants of Clovis

When Clovis died, he left four sons. The Germans followed the practice of dividing the property of the father equally among his male children. The Franks now applied this rule to the kingdom which Clovis left, and divided it just as though it were ordinary property. Each son received a portion of the kingdom, and each was independent of the others. This plan turned out very badly and caused a great deal of misery. None of the kings was ever satisfied with his own portion; but each wished to secure for himself the whole kingdom which Clovis had ruled.

So murders and civil wars became very common among these "Merovingian" princes, as they were called. Almost all of the descendants of Clovis died a violent death; or else their long hair,—which was their pride and the mark of their kingship,—was cut and they were forced into monasteries.

At one time, when one of the sons of Clovis died, his two brothers sent a message to their mother Clotilda saying:

"Send us our brother's children, that we may place them on the throne."

When the children were sent, a messenger came back to the grandmother, bearing a sword and a pair of shears, and telling her to choose whether the boys should be shorn or slain. In despair the old queen cried out:

"I would rather know that they were dead than shorn!"

Probably she did not mean this; but the pitiless uncles took her at her word. Two of the boys were cruelly slain; the third escaped from their hands, and to save his life he cut off his own hair and became a priest.

After a time the land of the Franks was divided into two divisions, and the people were called respectively East Franks and West Franks. Each land had a separate government. The West Franks gradually came to speak a language which was based on the old Latin language which the Romans had introduced into Gaul; and, long afterward, this grew into the French tongue of to-day. The East Franks, on the other hand, kept their old Germanic tongue, which finally developed into the German language as it is now spoken.

About a hundred years after the time of Clovis, two terrible women were queens in these lands. Their names were Fredegonda and Brunhilda; and their jealousy and hatred of each other caused them to commit many murders and stir up many wars. It is hard to say which of the two was the worse, but we feel some pity for Brunhilda because of her terrible end. She had murdered her grandchildren in order that she might keep the power in her own hands, and she was charged with causing the death of ten kings of Frankish race. But at last she fell into the hands of her enemies; and although she was an old woman of eighty years, she was put to death by being dragged at the heels of a wild horse. Her terrible rival had died some years before.

In many respects the laws of the Franks, and indeed of all the Germans, seem very strange to us. One of their strangest customs was that of the "feud," as it was called, and the "wergeld." Both of these had to do with such struggles as the one between Brunhilda and Fredegonda. In our day, and also among the Romans, if any one injured a man or killed him, the man or his family could go to law about it, and have the person who did the injury punished. But among the old Germans the courts of law had very little power, and many preferred to right their own wrongs. When a man was killed, his relatives would try to kill the slayer. Then the relatives of the slayer would try to protect him; and in this way a little war would arise between the two families. This was called a "feud"; and the struggle would go on until the number killed on each side equaled the number killed on the other.

By and by men began to see that this was a poor way of settling their grievances. Then it became the practice for the man who did the injury to pay a sum of money to the one who was injured; and the families helped in this, just as they had in the feud. When the payment was given for the slaying of a person it was styled "wergeld" or "man-money."

After this the feud was only used when the offender could not or would not pay the wergeld. Every man,—indeed every part of the body from a joint of the little finger up to the whole man,—came to have its price; and the wergeld of a Frank or of a Goth was about twice that of a Roman; and the wergeld of a person in the King's service was three times that of a simple freeman.

Another interesting thing about the old Germanic law was the way the trials were carried on. Let us suppose that a man is accused of stealing. We should at once try to find out whether any one had seen him commit the theft; that is, we should examine witnesses, and try to find out all the facts in the case. That was also the Roman way of doing things; but it was not the German way.

The Germans had several ways of trying cases, the most curious of which was the "ordeal." If they used this, they might force the man who was accused to plunge his hand into a pot of boiling water and pick up some small object from the bottom. Then the man's hand was wrapped up and sealed; and if in three days there was no mark of scalding, the man was declared innocent. In this way they left the decision of the case to God; for they thought that he would not permit an innocent man to suffer.

Merovingian king on an ox-cart

Besides this form of the ordeal, there were also others. In one of these the person accused had to carry a piece of red-hot iron in his hand for a certain distance. In another he was thrown, with hands and feet tied, into a running stream. If he floated, he was considered guilty; but if he sank, he was innocent, and must at once be pulled out. All of these forms of trial seem very absurd to us, but to men of the early Middle Ages they seemed perfectly natural; and they continued to be used until the thirteenth century.

In spite of the wickedness of the descendants of Clovis, and in spite of the divisions of the kingdom, the power of the Franks continued to increase. For about one hundred and seventy years the Merovingian kings were powerful rulers; then, for about one hundred years they gradually lost power until they became so unimportant that they are called "do-nothing" kings.

The rich estates which Clovis had left to his descendants were not wasted, through the reckless grants which the kings had made to their nobles. So poor were the kings that they could boast of but small estates and a scanty income; and when they wished to go from place to place they were forced to travel in an ox-cart, after the manner of the peasants. Now they had few followers, where before their warbands had numbered hundreds. All this made the kings so weak that the nobles no longer obeyed them. The government was left more and more to the charge of the kings' ministers; while the kings themselves were content to wear their long flowing hair, and sit upon the throne as figureheads.

The time had come when, indeed, the kings "did nothing." They reigned, but they did not rule.

Mohammed and the Mohammedans

While the descendants of Clovis were struggling with one another for his kingdom, and while the Church was gaining in wealth and in power, a danger was arising in the East that was to threaten both with ruin.

The city of Mecca

This danger was caused by the rise of a new religion among the Arabs. Arabia is a desert land for the most part; and the people gained their living by wandering with their camels and herds from oasis to oasis, or else by carrying on trade between India and the West, by means of caravans across the deserts. The people themselves were like grown-up children in many ways.

40

They had poetic minds, and impulsive and generous hearts; but they were ignorant and superstitious, and often very cruel. Up to this time they had never been united under one government, nor had they all believed in the same religion. Some tribes worshiped the stars of heaven, others worshiped "fetiches" of sticks and stones and others believed in gods or demons called "genii." If you have read the story of Aladdin and his wonderful lamp, in the "Arabian Nights," you will know what the "genii" were like. Arabia is so near Palestine that it will not surprise you to hear that the Arabs had also learned something of the religion of the Jews, and of the Christians. But until the seventh century after Christ, the Arabs remained, in spite of this, a rude and idolatrous people, without any faith or government which all acknowledged.

In the seventh century came a change. The Arabs then became a united people, under one government, and with one religion. And under the influence of this religion they came out from their deserts and conquered vast empires to the East and to the West, until it seemed as though the whole of the known world was to pass into their hands.

The man who brought about this change was named Mohammed. He belonged to a powerful tribe among the Arabs, but his father and mother had died before he was six years of age. He was then taken care of by his uncle, who was so poor that Mohammed was obliged to hire out as a shepherd boy, and do work that was usually done by slaves. When he was thirteen years old his uncle took him with a caravan to Damascus and other towns of Syria; and there the boy caught his first glimpses of the outside world. When he grew up he became manager for a wealthy widow who had many camels and sent out many caravans; and at last he won her love and respect, and she became his wife. When Mohammed established his new religion she became his first convert, and to the day of her death she was his most faithful friend and follower.

Mohammed had a dreamy and imaginative nature, and when he had become a man he thought much about religion. Every year he would go alone into the mountains near his home, and spend a month in fasting and prayer. At times he fell into a trance, and when he was restored he would tell of wonderful visions that his soul had seen while his body lay motionless on the earth.

When Mohammed was forty years old, a vision came to him of a mighty figure that called him by name and held an open book before him, saying, "Read!" Mohammed believed that this was the angel Gabriel, who came to him that he might establish a new religion, whose watchword should be:

"There is but one God, and Mohammed is his Prophet!"

When he began to preach the new faith, Mohammed found few converts at first. At the end of three years he had only forty followers. His teachings angered those who had charge of the idols of the old religions, and Mohammed was obliged at last to flee from the holy city of Mecca. This was in the year 622 A.D., and to this day the followers of Mohammed count time from this date, as we do from the birth of Christ.

After this Mohammed gained followers more rapidly, and he began to preach that the new religion must be spread by the sword. Warriors now came flocking into his camp from all directions. Within ten years after the flight from Mecca, all the tribes of Arabia had become his followers, and the idols had everywhere been broken to pieces. Then the Mohammedans turned to other nations, and everywhere they demanded that the people should believe in Mohammed, or pay tribute. If these demands were refused, they were put to death.

Mohammed could neither read nor write, but his sayings were written down by his companions. In this way a whole chestful of the sayings of the Prophet was preserved, written on scraps of paper, or parchment, on dried palm leaves, and even on the broad, flat shoulder-bones of sheep. After Mohammed's death these sayings were gathered together and formed into a book; in this way arose the "Koran," which is the bible of the Mohammedans.

Adam, Noah, Abraham, and Jesus were all recognized as prophets in the Koran; but Mohammed is regarded as the latest and greatest of all. The Koran teaches that those who believe in Mohammed, and live just lives, shall enter Paradise when they die. They will there dwell in beautiful gardens, where they shall never be burned by the rays of the sun, nor chilled by wintry winds; and there under flowering trees they shall recline forever, clad in silks and brocades, and fed by delicious fruits, which beautiful black-eyed maidens bring to them. To win Paradise the Mohammedan must follow certain rules. Five times a day he must pray with his face turned in the direction of the holy city Mecca; he must not gamble or drink wine; and during the holy month, when Mohammed fasted, he too must fast and pray. But the surest way to gain Paradise and all its joys, was to die in battle fighting for the Mohammedan faith. This teaching helps to explain why the Christians found the Mohammedans such fierce and reckless fighters.

Within a hundred years after the death of Mohammed, his followers had won an empire which stretched from the Indus River, in Asia, to the Red Sea, and from the Red Sea to the Atlantic Ocean. All of Southwestern Asia, and all of Northern Africa, were under their rule; and they were preparing to add Spain also, and perhaps all Europe, to the lands where the "call to prayer" was chanted.

In the year 711 A.D., a Mohammedan general named Tarik led the first army of Moors and Arabs across from Africa to Spain. Near where he landed was a huge mountain of rock, on which he built a fortress or castle; and from this name it is still called "Gible-Tarik," or Gibraltar, the mountain of Tarik.

Spain at this time was ruled by the West-Goths; but they were weakened by quarrels, and idleness, and were not able to resist the fierce Moors. Near a little river in Southern Spain the great battle was fought. For seven days the Christian Goths, under their King, Rodrigo, fought against the Mohammedan army; but still the battle was undecided. On the eighth day the Christians fled from the field, and Spain was left in the hands of the Mohammedans.

Long after that day an old Spanish poet sang of that battle in words like these:

"The hosts of Don Rodrigo were scattered in dismay,
When lost was the eight battle, nor heart nor hope had they;
He, when he saw that field was lost, and all his hope was flown,
He turned him from his flying host, and took his way alone.

"All stained and strewed with dust and blood, like to some smouldering brand
Plucked from the flame, Rodrigo showed; his sword was in his hand,
But it was hacked into a saw of dark and purple tint:
His jeweled mail had many a flaw, his helmet many a dint.

"He climbed into a hill-top, the highest he could see,
Thence all about of that wide rout his last long look took he;
He saw his royal banners, where they lay drenched and torn,
He heard the cry of victory, the Arab's shout of scorn.

"He looked for the brave captains that led the hosts of Spain,
But all were fled except the dead, and who could count the slain?
Where'er his eye could wander, all bloody was the plain,
And while thus he said, the tears he shed ran down his cheeks like rain:

"'Last night I was the King of Spain—to-day no king am I;
Last night fair castles held my train—to-night where shall I lie?
Last night a hundred pages did serve me on the knee—
To-night not one I call my own—not one pertains to me.'"

This battle destroyed the power of the West-Goths. It also marks the beginning of the rule of the Moors in Spain, which was to last until the time of Queen Isabella and Columbus.

The ease with which the Moors conquered Spain made them think it would be an easy thing to conquer Gaul also. So within a few years we find their armies crossing the Pyrenees to carry war into that land. But here they met the Franks, and that people was not so easy to overcome as the Goths had been.

The Mayors of the Palace

You have already seen how Clovis built up a strong kingdom in Gaul and Germany; and then how the power slipped away from the hands of his descendants, until they became mere "do-nothing" kings. An old Frankish writer says: "The kings had only the name, and nothing save means for meat and drink. They dwelt in a country house all the year, until the middle of May. Then they came forth to greet the people and be greeted by them, and to receive their gifts. After that they returned to their dwelling, where they remained until the next year."

The real power was now in the hands of the great nobles who acted as the King's ministers. The chief of these was called the "Mayor of the Palace"; and at the time when the Moors came into Spain this office was handed down from father to son in a powerful family, which possessed rich estates in the Rhine valley, and could command a multitude of warlike followers.

Three years after the Moors had crossed over into Spain, the old Mayor of the Palace died, and the office passed to his son Charles. This was a serious time for the kingdom of the Franks. Civil wars now broke out anew among the nobles; the Saxons from Germany broke into the kingdom from the North; and the Moors were pressing up from Spain into the very heart of France. The young Mayor of the Palace, however, proved equal to the occasion. The civil wars were brought to an end, and all the Frankish lands were brought under his rule. The heathen Saxons were driven back to their own country. Then, gathering an army from the whole kingdom, Charles marched, in the year 732, into Southern France to meet the Moors.

He found their army near the city of Tours, laden with the booty which they had taken. The Moors expected another victory as great as the one which had given them Spain; but they found their match in Charles and his Franks. All day long the battle raged. Twenty times the light-armed Moors, on their fleet horses, dashed into the ranks of the heavy-armed Franks; but each time Charles and his men stood firm, like a wall, and the enemy had to retreat. At last the Moors gave up the attempt; and when day dawned next morning the Franks found that they had slipped off in the night, leaving behind them their tents and all their rich booty.

This battle forever put an end to the conquests of the Moors in France. It was this battle also, perhaps, that gave Charles his second name, "Martel," or "the Hammer"; for, as an old writer tells us, "like a hammer breaks and dashes to pieces iron and steel, so Charles broke and dashed to pieces his enemies."

At all events, the fame which Charles Martel won by his actions, and the ability which he showed as a ruler, enabled him to leave his power to his two sons when he died. Again there was a war between the Mayors of the Palace and the nobles who ruled over portions of the kingdom, but again the Mayors of the Palace won. Then, when quiet was restored once more, the elder of the two sons of Charles gave over his power to his brother Pepin, and entered a monastery, in order that he might spend the rest of his years in the holy life of a monk.

This left Pepin (who was called "Pepin the Short") as the sole Mayor of the Palace. There was still a Merovingian prince who sat on the throne, but he was a "do-nothing" king, as so many had been before him; and he only said the words that he was told, and did the things that were given him to do.

Of course this could not go on forever. Every one was getting tired of it; and at last Pepin felt that the time had come when he might safely take the title of king. First, messengers were sent to the Pope to ask his opinion. The Pope was now eager to get the aid of the Franks against the Lombards in Italy; so he answered in the way that he knew would please Pepin.

"It is better," he said, "to give the title King to the person who actually has the power."

Then the weak Merovingian King was deposed. His long hair was cut, and he was forced to become a monk, and was shut out of sight in a monastery; and Pepin the Short was anointed with the sacred oil, and was crowned King in his place.

As long as Pepin lived, he ruled as a strong and just king. When he died, the crown went to his children, and after them to his children's children. In this way the crown of the Franks continued in the family of Pepin for more than two hundred years.

Charlemagne

Charles the Great, or Charlemagne, became King of the Franks when his father Pippin died. He was the greatest ruler of his time; and for hundreds of years after his death his influence continued to be felt in Western Europe. If Columbus had never been born, America would have been discovered just the same; and if Luther had never lived there would nevertheless have been a Reformation in the church. But if Charlemagne had never been King of the Franks, and made himself Emperor of the Holy Roman Empire,—as we shall see that he did,—the whole history of the Middle Ages would have been very different from what it actually was.

At first Charlemagne's brother ruled with him as King; but within three years the brother died, and then Charlemagne ruled as sole King of the Franks. He owed the power which he had largely to his father, and to his grandfather, Charles Martel; but Charlemagne used his power wisely and well, and greatly increased it. He put down the rebellions of the peoples who rose against the rule of the Franks; he defended the land against the Mohammedans of Spain and the heathen Germans of the North; he conquered new lands and new peoples. In addition he set up an improved system of government; and he did all that he could to encourage learning an make his people more civilized than they had been before.

When we read of all the things that Charlemagne did, we wonder that he was able to do so much. In the forty-six years that he was King he sent out more than fifty expeditions against different enemies; and in more than half of these he took the command himself. Charlemagne's wars, however, were not simply for plunder, or for more land, as so many of the earlier wars of the Franks had been. They were fought either to keep down the peoples whom the Franks had already conquered; or else to keep out new peoples who

45

were seeking to conquer the Franks. In both these objects Charlemagne was successful. The net result of his wars was that almost all those lands which had formerly been under the Emperors of the West, were now brought under the rule of the King of the Franks; and the peoples who lived in these lands, both the old inhabitants and the German newcomers, were allowed peaceably to live together and work out their own destiny.

The most stubborn enemy that Charlemagne had to fight was the Saxons. A portion of this people had settled in the island of Britain about three hundred years before; but many Saxon tribes still dwelt in the northern part of Germany. In Charlemagne's time they still worshipped Woden and Thor, and lived in much the same way that the Germans had done before the great migrations. It was part of Charlemagne's plan to make himself ruler of all the German nations; besides, there were constant quarrels along the border between the Saxons and the Franks. The result was that war was declared, and Charlemagne started out to conquer, to Christianize, and to civilize these heathen kinsmen. But it was a hard task; and the war lasted many years before it was ended. Again and again the Franks would march into the Saxon lands in summer and conquer the Saxon villages; but as soon as they withdrew for the winter the young warriors of the Saxons would come out from the swamps and forests to which they had retreated, and next year the work would have to be done over again.

After this had occurred several times, Charlemagne determined to make a terrible example. Forty-five hundred of the Saxon warriors who had rebelled and been captured were put to death by his orders, all in one day. This dreadful massacre was the worst thing that Charlemagne ever did; and it did not even succeed in terrifying the Saxons. Instead, it led to the hardest and bloodiest war of all, in which a chief named Widukind led on his countrymen to take vengeance for their murdered relatives and friends.

In the end Charlemagne and his Franks proved too strong for the Saxons. Widukind, at last, was obliged to surrender and be baptized, with all his followers. After that the resistance of the Saxons died away; and Charlemagne's treatment of the land was so wise that it became one of the strongest and most important parts of the kingdom.

Charlemagne also fought a number of times against the Arabs in Spain. He not only prevented them from settling in Southern France, as they had tried to do in the time of Charles Martel; but he won from them a strip of their own country south of the Pyrenees Mountains. In one of these wars, the rearguard of Charlemagne's army was cut off and slain by the mountain tribes in the narrow pass of Roncevalles. The leader of the Franks was Roland, while the leader of the enemy was called Bernardo.

Long after that day strange stories grew up and poets sang of the brave deeds of Roland, and of the mighty blasts which he gave on his hunting-horn, to warn Charlemagne of the danger to his army. Three blasts he blew, each so loud and terrible that the birds fell dead from the trees, and the enemy drew back in alarm. Charlemagne, many miles away, heard the call, and hastened to the rescue; but he came too late. An old song says:

"The day of Roncevalles was a dismal day for you,
Ye men of France, for there the lance of King Charles was broke in two;
Ye well may curse that rueful field, for many a noble peer
In fray or fight the dust did bite beneath Bernardo's spear."

In most of his wars Charlemagne was successful; and the stories about him told rather of his glory and his might than of his defeats.

One of his most important conquests was that of the Lombards, in Northern Italy. Nearly a century afterward, an old monk wrote the story of this war as he had heard it from his father. Desiderius, the King of the Lombards, had offended the Pope, and the Pope appealed to Charlemagne for aid. When Charlemagne marched his army over the Alps into Italy, the Lombard King shut himself up in his capital, Pavia. There he had with him, according to the story, one of Charlemagne's nobles named Otker, who had offended the dread King and fled from him.

"Now when they heard of the approach of the terrible Charles," writes this old monk, "they climbed up into a high tower, whence they could see in all directions. When the advance guard appeared, Desiderius said to Otker: 'Is Charles with this great army, do you think?' And he answered: 'Not yet.' When he saw the main army, gathered from the whole broad empire, Desiderius said with confidence: 'Surely the victorious Charles is with these troops.' But Otker answered: 'Not yet, not yet.'

"Then Desiderius began to be troubled, and said: 'What shall we do if still more come with him?' Otker answered: 'You will soon see how he will come; but what will become of us, I know not.' And, behold, while they were speaking, appeared the servants of Charles's household, a never-resting multitude. 'That is Charles,' said the terrified Desiderius. But Otker said: 'Not yet, not yet.' Then appeared the bishops and the abbots, and the chaplains with their companions. When he beheld these the Lombard prince, dazed with fear and longing for death, stammered out these words: 'Let us go down and hide in the earth before the wrath of so terrible an enemy!' But Otker, who in better times had known well the power and the arms of the great Charles, answered: 'When you see a harvest of steel waving in the fields, and the rivers dashing steel-black waves against the city walls, then you may believe Charles is coming.'

"Scarcely had he spoken when there appeared in the North and West a dark cloud, as it were, which wrapped the clear day in most dreadful shadow. But as it drew nearer, there flashed upon the besieged from the gleaming weapons a day that was more terrible for them than any night. Then they saw him,—Charles,—the man of steel; his arms covered with plates of steel, his iron breast and his broad shoulders protected by steel armor. His left hand carried aloft the iron lance, for his right was always ready for the victorious sword. His thighs, which others leave uncovered in order more easily to mount their horses, were covered on the outside with iron scales. The leg-pieces of steel were common to the whole army. His shield was all of steel, and his horse was iron in color and in spirit.

"This armor all who rode before him, by his side, or who followed him,—in fact, the whole army,—had tried to imitate as closely as possible. Steel filled the fields and roads. The rays of the sun were reflected from gleaming steel. The people, paralyzed by fear, did homage to the bristling steel; the fear of the steel pierced down deep into the earth. 'Alas, the steel!' 'Alas, the steel!' cried the inhabitants confusedly. The mighty walls trembled before the steel, and the courage of youths fled before the steel of the aged.

"And all this, which I have told with all too many words, the truthful seer Otker saw with one swift look, and said to Desiderius: 'There you have Charles, whom you have so long desired!' And with these words he fell to the ground like one dead."

In this war Charlemagne was completely victorious. Desiderius ceased to be King of the Lombards, and Charlemagne became King in his place. For centuries after that Charlemagne's successors continued to wear "the iron crown of Italy," which the great King of the Franks had won from Desiderius.

One of the results of the conquest of the Lombards was that Charlemagne was brought into closer relations with the Pope. The Emperor of the East still claimed to rule over Italy; but his rule was feeble, and only a small part of the peninsula was now in the hands of his officers. The real power in Italy had passed into the hands of the King of the Franks; and the question now was, whether the Pope should be under his rule as he had been under that of the Eastern Emperors.

Two things made this question harder to decide. One was that Charle-magne, following the example of his father Pippin, had given to the Pope a large number of the cities and villages which he had conquered in Italy. The other was that the Pope, on Christmas day of the year 800, placed a crown on Charlemagne's head as he knelt in prayer in St. Peter's church at Rome, and proclaimed him Emperor.

Charlemagne had gone to Rome to aid the Pope against rebellious Romans, and remained for the celebration of Christmas. On that day, as Charlemagne's secretary tells us, "the King went to mass at St. Peter's, and as he knelt in prayer before the alter, the Pope set a crown upon his head. Then the Roman people cried aloud: 'Long life and victory to the mighty Charles, the great and peaceful Emperor of the Romans, who is crowned of God!'" He adds that later Charlemagne declared "that he would not have set foot in the church that day, although it was a great feast-day, if he could have foreseen the design of the Pope." Nevertheless, Charlemagne accepted the new title, and prized it higher than his old title of King.

When Charlemagne gave those cities and villages to the Pope, did it mean that he gave up the right to rule there, and turned the power over to the Pope, so that the latter became the Prince in these places? And when the

Pope crowned Charlemagne as Emperor, did that mean that the Pope could set up and pull down emperors whenever he pleased?

These are very hard questions to answer; but they are very important questions to understand. Upon the answers given to them would depend the decision whether the Pope was above the Emperor, or the Emperor above the Pope; and this was a question about which men fought for hundreds of years.

We may also ask, What was this Empire of which Charlemagne became Emperor on that Christmas morning?

The name which men give to it is "the Holy Roman Empire of the German Nation." They thought of it as a revival of the old Roman Empire of the East, which had come to an end more than three hundred years before. They called it the *Holy* Roman Empire, to show how great a part the Church, and especially the Pope, played in it; and they added the words, *of the German Nation*, because it was the new and vigorous peoples who had come from the North who now supplied its strength. Though Charlemagne as Emperor ruled only over the peoples who had obeyed him as King, still men felt that his position now was higher, and his authority greater, than it had been before. For now his power was linked with the majestic history of Rome, and was given a more solemn sanction by the Church.

In this way the crowning of Charlemagne as Emperor was an event of very great importance. For a thousand years after that day, the office of Emperor in the West continued to exist; and for a good part of this time it was one of the most powerful means of holding peoples of Western Europe together in one family of nations, and preventing them from growing wholly unlike and hostile to one another. We may truly say that a new age commences in Europe, when force alone no longer rules, and when great ideas, such as the idea of the Church and of the Empire, begin to play a part amid the strife of nations.

To govern the wide territories which were under his rule, Charlemagne kept up the "counts" or local rulers that he found established in different parts of his Empire. Over these he set higher rulers, called *Missi* or "messengers," who were to travel about the country, seeing everything and reporting everything to the King.

Twice a year, in the spring and in the autumn, the nobles of the land were called together to consult with him, and assist him in making laws for the kingdom. These assemblies would continue for several days, according to the importance of the business. While they lasted, the nobles would come and go from the King's palace, proposing laws to the their followers, and carrying back their assent. The King's will decided everything; the nobles advised; their followers merely assented to what was proposed.

If the weather was fine, the assembly met in the open air; but if it was not, then the meetings took place in churches and other buildings. The King, meanwhile, was busy receiving presents, talking with the most important men, especially those who dwelt at a distance from his court, and hearing what his nobles and officials had to report to him concerning any part of the kingdom. This last Charlemagne considered very important. As an old writer says:

"The King wished to know whether, in any part or any corner of the kingdom, the people murmured or were troubled, and what was the cause of their troubles. Also he wished to know if any of the conquered peoples thought of rebelling, or if any of those who were still independent threatened the kingdom with an attack. And upon all these matters, wherever a danger or a disturbance arose, his chief questions were concerned with its motives or its cause."

Besides being a great warrior and a great ruler, Charlemagne was also a great friend of learning and education. He loved to gather about him learned men from all parts of the world. In this "Palace School," as it was called, the King and his wise men discussed learned questions. Charlemagne himself learned to read only after he was a grown man; and in spite of all his efforts he never succeeded in learning to write. This made him all the more anxious that the bright lads of his kingdom should have the advantages which he lacked. So he founded schools in the monasteries and bishoprics; in this way he hoped to get learned men for offices in the Church and State. The rude, fighting men of that day, however, looked upon learning with contempt; and many noble youths in the schools neglected their books for hawking and warlike exercises.

The old monk who tell us how Charles overcame King Desiderius, also tells us of the Emperor's wrath when he found the boys of one school going on in this fashion. The boys of low and middle station had been faithful; and when they presented their compositions and poems to the King, he said:

"Many thanks, my sons, that you have taken such pains to carry out my orders to the best of your ability. Try now to do better still, and I will give you as reward splendid bishoprics, and make you rulers over monasteries, and you shall be highly honored in my sight."

But to the high-born boys, who had played while the others worked, he cried out in wrath:

"You sons of princes, you pretty and dainty little gentlemen, who count upon your birth and your wealth! You have disregarded my orders and your own reputations; you have neglected your studies and spent your time in games and idleness, or in foolish occupations! I care little for your noble birth, and your pretty looks, though others think them so fine! And let me promise you this: if you do not make haste to recover what you have lost by your neglect, you need never think to get any favors from Charles!"

In many other ways, besides those which we have mentioned, Charlemagne did a great work for the peoples over whom he ruled, and laid the foundations on which the ages that came after builded. In the troubled times that followed his death much of his work seemed to be swept away; but this was only in seeming, for the most important parts of it lived and still live in the governments and civilization of the world.

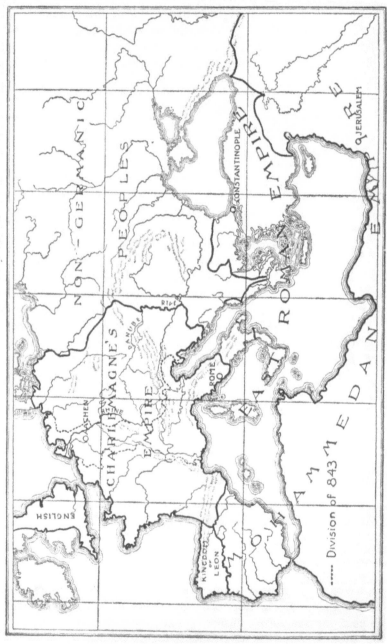

Map of Charlemagne's Empire

Before taking leave of this great King, perhaps you would like to know what he looked like, and how he lived. One of the learned men of his court has left a good description of him. "He was tall and stoutly built," he says, "his height being just seven times the length of his own foot. His head was round, his eyes large and lively, his nose somewhat above the common size, and his expression bright and cheerful. Whether he stood or sat, his form was full of dignity; for the good proportion and grace of his body prevented the observer from noticing that his neck was rather short and his person rather too fleshy." He was very active, this same writer tells us, and delighted in riding and hunting, and was skilled in swimming. It was, indeed, because of its natural warm baths that he made his favorite residence and capital at Aachen (The Frank Aix-la-Chapelle). He always wore the Frankish dress; but on days of state he added to this an embroidered cloak and jeweled crown, and carried a sword with a jeweled hilt. The name (Charlemagne), by which we know him, is French, but the King himself, in speech, dress, and habits, was a thoroughly German king, and ruled over a thoroughly German people.

Descendants of Charlemagne

Upon the death of Charlemagne, his Empire passed to his son Louis. This ruler is sometimes called "Louis the Pious," because he was so friendly to the Church; and sometimes "Louis the Good-natured," because he was so easy-going and allowed himself to be guided by his wife and his favorites. Under his weak rule the Empire lost much of the strength that it had possessed under Charlemagne.

After Louis's death, it was still further weakened. His sons had begun fighting for the kingdom even while their father lived. After his death they fought a great battle in which troops of all the Frankish lands took part. The old writers describe this as a terrible struggle,—more terrible than any since Attila and his Huns were driven back by the Romans and the Goths, or the Moors were defeated by Charles Martel. Those battles had been fought by the Christians against peoples who were not Christians; but now Christians fought against Christians, Franks against Franks.

"May the day of that battle be accursed!" wrote a writer who himself took part in the struggle. "May it never more be counted among the days of the year, but be wiped out from all remembrance! May it lack the light of the sun, and have neither dawning nor twilight! May that night also be accursed; that terrible night in which so many brave and skillful warriors met their deaths! Never was there a worse slaughter! Men fell in lakes of blood; and the garments of the dead whitened the whole field."

As a result of this battle, the three sons of Louis agreed to divide the kingdom among them. (1) Charles, the youngest son, got the western part, and this in course of time grew into the kingdom of France. (2) Ludwig, the second son, got the land lying east and north of the Rhine River and Alps Mountains; and this region in time became the kingdom of Germany. (3) Lothair, the eldest son, got Italy, and a long narrow strip which lay between Charles's portion on the West and Ludwig's portion on the East; and with it he received the title of Emperor. This "middle strip" was long and awkwardly shaped, and there was so little to bind the people together that it never grew into a permanent kingdom. Before many years had gone by, it passed into the hands of the rulers of France and Germany, and the only thing that remained to show its former rule was the name "Lotharingia" or "Lorraine," which is still given to the northern part of it.

This division of the kingdom tended, of course, to make the Frankish power weaker. Other things, too, contributed to this end. The Carolingian princes (as the descendants of Charles are called) were not nearly as strong rulers as their great forefather had been, and besides they continued the practice of dividing the kingdoms among all the sons whenever a king died. So the kingdoms grew ever smaller and weaker.

New enemies, moreover, had now arisen to trouble the land, and make the task of governing it more difficult. The Moors of Spain and Africa were going far into the heart of France and Italy in their search for plunder and slaves. On the North and West fleets of Viking ships, laden with fierce Northmen from Denmark and Norway, were landing upon the coast, or ascending in their light vessels far up the rivers, plundering, killing, and burning. And from the East the Hungarians—a new race, of close kin to the old Huns— were now advancing year after year up the Danube valley, into Germany, into Italy, into France, carrying everywhere terror and dismay.

Since the kings of this period were too weak to protect the land against attack, the people were obliged to look after their own defence. The result was that rich and powerful landowners began to build great gloomy towers and castles as a protection against these raids. In course of time every lofty hill-top, every cliff, every island in the great rivers, came to have a castle, where the lord and his followers might find protection against their enemies. There was now no power in the state either to protect or to punish its subjects; so these lords not only used their castles as a defence against the Hungarians and other enemies, but often themselves oppressed their neighbors. From their strongholds they would sally forth to misuse the peasants of the country around, or to plunder merchants travelling from town to town.

Everything was fallen into confusion; and it seemed as if the time told of in the Bible, when "every man did that which seemed good in his own eyes," had again come upon earth.

Rise of Feudalism

There seemed to be only one remedy against these evils for the ordinary freeman. This was to give up his independence, and get the lord of some castle to agree to protect him against all other enemies. That, in fact, is just what we find going on in this period. Men everywhere were giving up their *independence*, and becoming the *dependents* of some great man who took them under his protection.

When a freeman wished to "commend himself," as it was called, to the protection of a lord, he went down on his knees before him, put his hands between the hands of the lord, and swore to be "his man" — that is, to serve him. Then the lord raised his "vassal," as the man was thenceforth called, and gave him the kiss of peace. This was called "doing homage" to the lord. Next the vassal swore to be faithful to his lord in all things; this was the "oath of fealty."

If the man had land in his own right, he usually gave it up to the lord, and the lord then gave him back the *use* of it.

A vassal doing homage to his lord

If he had no land before, the lord granted him the use of some of his own land; and a lance, or a twig, was given him at the time he did homage, in sign of this. Thenceforth the lord was the real owner of the land, but the vassal had the use of it till his death. When he died, his son would do homage and swear fealty to the lord, and then he would be given the land his father held. Such a piece of land was called a "benefice" or a "fief," and the name which is given to the whole system is "feudalism," or the "feudal system."

As a result of this system the ordinary freemen gained the protection which they so much needed and the state could no longer furnish. Thenceforth they had a place of refuge, in the lord's castle, to which they could flee

55

when robber bands appeared; and they also had a powerful protector to defend them against the attacks of other lords.

"But," you may ask, "what good was all this to the lord of the castle? Why was he willing to admit these men to become his vassals, and even grant them parts of his own lands as benefices?" That is a question which is easily answered. The lord needed *men* to help him guard his castle, and fight his battles; and that was what the vassals supplied. Every year they might be called upon to serve their lord as armored knights for forty days in the field, besides rendering him other services. In this way the lord obtained military followers, who were closely bound to him by ties of homage and fealty; and the more vassals he had, the more powerful he became.

The lords themselves in turn often became the vassals of some greater lord above them, and bound themselves to bring all of *their* followers to serve him, when called upon to do so. In the completed system, the king of the land stood at the head; then under him were *his* vassals, and under them were *their* vassals,—and so on until we come down to the peasants. They were not looked upon as worthy to be the *vassals* of anybody; they were called "serfs" or "villains," and had to till the soil, and raise the food which supported all the classes above them.

Lord and dependents feasting

From what you have been told you might think that feudalism was an organization only for fighting; but it was something more than this. It came to be an organization for governing the land as well. The power of the kings became so weak that the feudal nobles were able finally to take into their own hands most things that the head of the state ought to have done. In this way it came about that the feudal lords had the right to make war, coin money, make laws, and hold courts in their fiefs. Sometimes they had their own gallows on which to hang offenders. The power that ought to have been in the hands of the head of the state was thus split up into many bits, and each of these great lords had part of it.

The growth of the feudal system was going on everywhere in Western Europe from about the eighth to the eleventh centuries. It grew slowly, but it grew surely; for in the weakened condition of the state it was the form of organization that best met the needs of the people. So everywhere,—in Spain, in France, in England, in Germany, and in Italy—we find the feudal castles arising; and men everywhere gave up their free land, received it back as fiefs, and became the vassals of lords above them.

The existence of feudalism is one of the most important facts about the Middle Ages. It is this which makes the government of that period so different from the governments of Greece and Rome, and also from the governments of to-day. Feudalism, moreover, led to other important changes. In the Church it made the abbots and bishops the vassals of the kings and nobles for the land which the Church held; and since vassals owed military service, the bishops and abbots often became more like feudal warriors than mild and holy servants of Christ. Because the chief business of vassals and lords was fighting, much attention was paid to arms and armor, and to training for war. In this way arose the wonderful coats of mail and suits of armor of the Middle Ages; in this way also arose the long training which one had to go through to become a knight, and the exciting "tournaments" in which the knights tried their skill against one another.

In another chapter is an account of The Life of the Castle; we tell you of these things here only that you may see how truly we may say of this period, that it was indeed the Feudal Age, as it is sometimes called. Especially is this true of the eleventh, twelfth, and thirteenth centuries. It is in those centuries preeminently that we find feudalism grown into a complete system, and ruling the whole life of the lands which the German conquerors had won from the Roman Empire.

Deeds of the Northmen

One of the things which helped the growth of feudalism was the coming of the Northmen into Southern Europe.

The Northmen were a sturdy people who dwelt about the Baltic Sea, in the lands which their descendants—the Danes, Norwegians, and Swedes—still occupy. There they had dwelt as long as we have any record of them. While the other Germans were seeking new homes in the fifth and sixth centuries, the Northmen had remained quietly at home worshiping the old gods, and gaining a scanty living from their herds and fields, and from the sea. They were so far away from Rome that only faint reports reached them of the stirring events that were taking place in the Roman lands. For four hundred years after the Goths had crossed the frontier, the Northmen remained quiet.

But at last Charlemagne's conquest of the Saxons brought Christianity and the Frankish rule close to their doors. Traders and missionaries now began to come among them; from them they learned of the rich and beautiful lands which lay to the South, and their minds were dazzled by the thought of the easy victories which were to be won there.

When finally the Northmen came into the southern lands, they came, not by land, as the earlier invaders had done, but by sea. The rocky islands, the bold cliffs, and the narrow valleys of the Scandinavian lands did not tempt men to agriculture. On the other hand, the sea invited them to voyage forth and seek adventures on its waters. The Northmen, therefore, had become

A Viking ship

bold sailors; and in their long, many-oared ships, they now dared the storms of heaven and the wrath of man, to sail wherever there was booty to be had or glory to be gained. They called themselves "Viking," which means "men from the viks," or creeks of Scandinavia. Even in Charlemagne's time the Northmen had begun to trouble the southern lands.

"One day, while Charlemagne tarried in a city of Southern Gaul," says an old writer, "a few Scandinavian boats came to plunder even within the harbor of the city. Some thought at first that they were Jewish merchants; others believed that they were from Northern Africa, or were traders from Brittany. But Charlemagne recognized them by the fleetness of their ships.

'These are not merchants,' he said, 'but cruel enemies.'

When the ships were pursued, they quickly disappeared. Then the Emperor, rising from the table where he sat, went to the window which looked towards the East, and remained there a long time, his eyes filled with tears. No one ventured to question him; but at last he said:

'Do you know, my faithful friends, why I weep so bitterly? It is not because I fear that these men should annoy me by their wretched acts of piracy. But I am deeply afflicted because during my lifetime they have come so near these shores; and I am tormented by a great grief when I think of the woes they will inflict upon my successors and the whole nation.'"

Before Charlemagne was dead, indeed, these hardy wanderers began to fulfill his prophecy; and after he was gone the evil increased rapidly. Now the Viking ships came by scores and hundreds, where before they had come singly and in dozens. The whole of Christendom suffered from them. They plundered the shores alike of Germany, France, England, Scotland, Ireland, Spain and Italy. With their light vessels they would enter the river mouths, and row as far into the heart of the country as they could. Then they would seize horses, and on these ride far and wide. They loved most of all to attack the churches and monasteries. They cared nothing for the Christian God, for they were still heathen; and in the churches were rich gold and silver vessels, and fine embroidered cloths. It was easier, also, to capture a church or a monastery than it was a castle, for the priests and monks were not fighting men. And if any resisted these fierce heathen, they were pierced with arrows, or cloven with their swords.

One of the most famous Vikings was named Hastings. Some say that he was not a Northman at all, but a French peasant, who had joined the sea-rovers. At all events, he was very strong, brave, and cunning, and became one of their most famous leaders. We first meet with him while Louis the Pious was King; for nearly fifty years after this he was busy plundering towns and wasting the country in different lands. Now we find him in France; now he is in Frisia, just north of France; now he is in England; now he is on the shores of Spain.

On one voyage Hastings sailed around the Spanish peninsula and entered the Mediterranean Sea. There he plundered Southern France, Africa, and Italy. He wished especially to plunder Rome, as Alaric and the Vandal king had done before him. But he knew more about fighting than he did about geography. On the coast of Italy, north of Rome, lay a little city called Luna, and Hastings mistook its marble palaces and churches for the buildings of Rome. Even the walls of Luna, however, were too strong to be taken by force; so he was obliged to use a trick. He sent a messenger into the city saying that he had not come to make war, but was dying and wished to be baptized a Christian. The bishop and rulers of the city were pleased at this, and Hastings was baptized as he wished. Then the next day word was brought from the ships that their leader was dead, and they wished him to be buried in the church of the city. There seemed no harm in this request, so the rulers gave their consent. Hastings, with his weapons lying by his side, was brought within the walls, and with him came some of his best warriors, as mourners. While the people of the city went with the funeral party to the church, the rest of the Northmen landed from their ships and slipped through the unguarded gate. Then Hastings suddenly seized his weapons and sprang from the couch where he lay; at once his followers fell upon the people, and in this way the town was soon won.

At first the Northmen came only during the summer season, sailing home when the winter storms were due. Before long, however, they began to spend the winter also in Christian lands. They would seize upon an island lying off the coast at a river's mouth; and from this as headquarters they would go forth at all times of the year to ravage the land. For many years this prayer was regularly used in the churches: "From the fury of the Northmen, good Lord, deliver us."

Count Odo bringing aid to Paris

The struggle lasted for a long time. In France, within fifty years after Charlemagne's death, Paris had fallen three times. At first the weak kings tried to buy off the Northmen with gifts of money. But such gifts only made them greedy for more; and payment had to be made again and again. Then the nobles and the cities took the defence into their own hands. In addition to the castles which the nobles were building, the cities began to fortify bridges over the rivers, so that they could keep the pirate ships from ascending the streams.

The most famous struggle of all came at Paris in the year 886. This city was not yet the capital of France, but its situation already made it important. It was built on a low island in the Seine, with a fortified bridge connecting it with each bank. When the Northmen came up the river in that year, the governor of the city, Count Odo, and the bishop, encouraged the people to resist. The Viking ships numbered seven hundred, and they carried an army of 40,000 men; but for eleven months the city held out, and in spite of the weakness and cowardice of the King, the Northmen at last were obliged to withdraw.

The family of this Count Odo had already won great honor in warring against the Northmen. His father, Robert the Strong, had fallen, after many victories, fighting against the pirate Hastings. The brave defence of Paris now made Odo more powerful than ever, and men began to think how much worthier he was of the crown than the weak Carolingians. So the cowardly King who was then ruling was set aside, and Count Odo was chosen King in his place.

After Odo's death the Carolingians regained the throne, but their hold upon it was weaker than ever. For about a hundred years the family of Odo continued to be the rivals of the Carolingians. Then in 987, another descendant of Robert the Strong seized the throne, and this time the change of rulers was permanent. From that date, for more than eight hundred years, all of the kings of France were descendants of this great family; and their rule did not cease until the kingship came to an end in France, and a republic was set up in its place (1792).

Twenty-five years after the great siege of Paris, a band of Northmen secured such a footing in France that it was never possible afterwards to drive them forth. Their leader was a man of enormous size, strength, and courage; his name was Rolf (or Rollo), and they called him "the Ganger," which meant "the Walker." Like Hastings, he was for nearly fifty years a sea-king, plundering Frisia, England, Scotland, and France. At the great siege of Paris, he was one of the chiefs. Unlike Hastings, however, Rolf was something more than a mere pirate and robber. When he captured a town, he strengthened its walls, and rebuilt its churches, and sought to rule over it as a conquering prince.

In this way he came to possess a number of towns which lay north and south of the mouth of the river Seine. At last, in the year 911, he secured a grant from the King of France to a wide stretch of country in that region, with the title of Duke. This grant was made on three conditions. First, he must settle his Northmen there and leave the rest of the country at peace; second, he must become a Christian; and third, he must do homage to the French King as his feudal lord. This last condition was very distasteful to Duke Rolf, and he could scarcely be induced to place his hands between the hands of the King, as was required. When he was told to kneel down and kiss the foot of the King, as was the custom, he refused, and calling one of his followers, commanded him to do it. This bold Northman, however, had no more liking for the deed than his chief; and when he raised the King's foot to touch it to his lips, he toppled the King over on his back!

In Normandy,—as his land was called,—Duke Rolf speedily showed that he was as good a ruler as he was a fighter. His followers settled down quietly, under his stern rule, and became landlords and cultivators of the soil. Before he died, it is said that gold rings could be hung on the limbs of the trees, and no one would touch them. The Northmen learned rapidly in other ways too. They followed the lead of their Duke in being baptized, and soon all were Christians. They also laid aside their old speech and law, and in less than a hundred years the fierce sea-rovers had become as good Frenchmen, in speech and everything else, as could be found in the kingdom. About the only thing to mark the difference between these Normans, as they were called, and the rest of the French, was their greater energy, their skill in governing, and their fondness for the sea and adventure.

Proof that they had not lost their energy or military skill was given in events which took place in the eleventh century. Within a little more than a hundred years after Duke Rolf and his followers were established in France, their descendants began to send forth new bands of conquerors. By accident their attention was turned to Sicily and the southern part of Italy. Soon the greater part of these lands was conquered from the Greeks and Saracens, and a Norman kingdom was established there called the kingdom of the Two Sicilies.

This is not nearly all of the great deeds the Northmen and their descendants performed at this time; but we can only mention a few of the others. As every American boy and girl knows, the Northmen settled Iceland and Greenland, and discovered America long before Columbus was born. Twice bands of them attacked the city of Constantinople; and after that they entered the service of the Greek Emperor, and for centuries made up his faithful bodyguard. In the far North, they made settlements in Russia, and gave a line of rulers to the Great Russian Empire. And when the Crusaders set out to win Jerusalem from the infidels, the Normans of France, England, and Sicily took the leading part in these movements also.

These old Northmen were truly a wonderful people, and their coming into the Christian lands did much to make the southern nations stronger and more energetic than they would otherwise have been.

England in the Middle Ages

The British Isles were among the lands which suffered most from the raids of the Viking Northmen, and it was there also that the Normans of France made their greatest conquest.

In the days when Rome was spreading her rule about the Mediterranean Sea, the larger of these islands was called Britain, from its inhabitants, the Britons, who were akin to the Gauls of the Continent. Some time after the Romans had conquered Gaul, Britain also was added to their Empire and was ruled by the Romans for about three hundred and fifty years. But when the Empire had grown weak and the German barbarians began to over-run Italy, Rome was obliged to withdraw her legions from Britain, and that island was then left to govern and defend itself.

The Britons, however, had lived so long under Roman rule that, by this time, they had almost forgotten how to fight. So, when wild tribes from Ireland and Scotland came to attack them, the Britons were in an evil situation. At one time they wrote a letter to the Roman commander in Gaul, in which they said:

"The barbarians drive us to the sea; the sea throws us back on the barbarians. Thus two modes of death await us: we are either slain, or drowned."

Also, roving bands of Germans, called Angles and Saxons, now began to trouble the shores of Britain, coming in their swift pirate ships much as the Northmen were to do four hundred years later. When the Britons found that the Romans were not able to help them, they asked a band of these sea-rovers to aid them against their other enemies, promising them rich rewards (449 A.D.). When once the Angles and Saxons had secured a footing, they proceeded to conquer the island for themselves. In this way the Angles and Saxons won for themselves the fairest portion of the land. From the name of the first of these peoples, it came to be called "Angle-land" or England. It was only after two centuries of hard fighting, however, that the conquest was completed. In the western part of the island the Britons long kept their independence; and there, under the name of "Welsh," as they were styled by the new-comers (a word which meant foreigners), they continued for hundreds of years to use their own language, to follow their own laws, and to obey their own princes.

Meanwhile the "English," as the descendants of the Angles and Saxons are called, settled down into a num¬ber of little kingdoms. You have already read how captive boys from one of these kingdoms excited the pity of Pope Gregory when he saw them exposed for sale in the slave market at Rome, and how this led him to send the monk Au¬gustine to England, to convert these new-comers. The English became Christians and grew more civilized, and finally their little kingdoms were joined together under the rule of a single king.

But now they, in turn, were exposed to the danger of conquest; for like the Britons before them the English had, through long years of peace, lost much of their former warlike ability. The new enemy was the Northmen, whose deeds we have described in the preceding chapter. Little by little they overran the island, plundering and destroying monasteries and churches, until only the south-western part of the island was still unconquered. But there they were met by a young English King who stopped their conquests and saved his people from ruin at their hands.

This was the English national hero. Alfred, whom later ages called "Alfred the Truth-Teller" and "England's Darling." When he was a boy his mother one day said to him and his brothers:

"Do you see this little book, with its clear black writing, and the beautiful letter at the beginning, painted in red, blue, and gold? It shall belong to the one who first learns its songs."

Books were precious things in those days, for printing was not yet invented and they must be made slowly and painfully by writing the letters with a pen. So Alfred exclaimed eagerly:

"Mother, will you really give that beautiful book to me if I learn it first?"

"Yes," she replied, "I really will."

So Alfred set to work, with the aid of his teacher; and long before his brothers had mastered it, he learned to repeat the verses. He thus not only earned the prize, but in doing it he showed the love of learning and quickness of mind which made him noted in after years.

The first seven years of Alfred's rule as King were taken up with fighting the Northmen. At one time he was obliged to take refuge on a small island amid swamps, where he found shelter in a herdsman's hut, and was scolded by the herdsman's wife (who did not know who he was) for letting some coarse cakes burn which she was baking before the fire. An old song represents the woman as saying:

> Can't you mind the cakes, man?
> And don't you see them burnt?
> I'm bound you'll eat them fast enough,
> As soon as 'tis the turn.

In the end Alfred defeated the Northmen in a great battle, and forced their king to make peace. The remainder of his reign was given up to improving education and bettering the condition of his people. He was "the wisest, best, and greatest King that ever reigned in England," and the good effects of his rule lasted long after he was gone.

But, after a time, the rule came again into the hands of weak kings, and again Northmen overran the land.

Canute, King of Denmark and Norway, conquered England, and was recognized as King by all that land. Fortunately the Northmen were now Christians and more civilized than they had been in Alfred's day; and Canute ruled England as a strong and able King for nearly twenty years.

After Canute's death there was again trouble for a number of years. First his unworthy sons ruled after him; and when their short reigns were at an end, a well meaning but weak King of the old English line, named Edward, was placed on the throne. His mother was a Norman, and he himself had spent a part of his youth in Normandy, where the descendants of the Northmen were now the most energetic and enlightened people of France. King Edward was so fond of the Normans that he invited many of them to come over into his kingdom, where he showed them such favor that it aroused the jealousy of the English and led to many conflicts. When Edward died, in the year 1066, without leaving a son to succeed him, the English chose as King a nobleman named Harold, who had taken a chief part in resisting those Norman favorites.

The Duke of Normandy at this time was a strong ruler named William, who had already done great things and was looking about for an opportunity to do greater ones. He claimed that King Edward had promised him the throne when, at one time, he had visited him in England; and also that Harold, who had taken Edward's place, had sworn never to become king. So, with a great army of Normans and Frenchmen, and with a banner blessed by the Pope, William landed on the shores of England to claim the throne.

Normans landing in England

At a hill called Senlac, not far from the town of Hastings, the Normans found King Harold and his Englishmen awaiting them. For a time it looked as though the Normans would be defeated, for the English ranks held firm and could not be broken. Three horses were killed under William, but he escaped without injury. At one time the cry was raised, "The Duke is down!" and the Normans began to give way. But William tore off his helmet that they might better see his face, and cried:

"I live, and by God's help shall have the victory!"

After a time William ordered his men to pretend to flee, in order to draw the English from their strong position. This move succeeded in part, but still the battle went on. William next ordered that a volley of arrows be shot high in the air, and one of these in falling struck Harold in the eye and slew him. Then the Normans easily won the battle.

After this William got possession of all England, and was accepted by the people as their King. He is known in history as William the Conqueror. He was a strong and able ruler, and he and his descendants knew how to keep what their energy and valor had won. From that day to this, every king or queen who has ruled over England has been a descendant of this Norman Duke. His Conquest was the greatest feat which the Normans accomplished, and it is one of the most important events in the history of the Middle Ages.

The First Crusade

The period of the Crusades lasts from the year 1095 to the year 1270. In the great movement included between these dates we find, for the first time, practically the whole of Europe acting together for one end. And it was not only the rulers who were concerned; priests and kings, nobles, townsmen and peasants, alike took arms against the infidel. The story of the Crusades, therefore, is one of the most important and interesting parts of medieval history. Nothing can better show what the Middle Ages were like; and nothing helped more than they did to bring the Middle Ages to their end.

The object of this movement was to bring Palestine, where Christ had lived and died, again under the rule of Christians. Until the Arabs began their conquests in the seventh century, the land had been ruled by the Eastern Emperors. Even after the religion of Mohammed was established side by side with that of Christ, the Christians did not at first feel so badly about it. They were too busy at home, fighting Northmen and Hungarians, and settling the institutions under which they were to live, to give much attention to things so far way. Besides, the Arabs respected the holy places of the Christians, and allowed pilgrims to Jerusalem to come and go without harm or hindrance.

But about thirty years before William the Norman conquered England, a new race appeared in the East. The Turks, who were a rude fierce people from Central Asia, of close kin to the old Huns, conquered the Arabs; and the treatment of the Christian was thenceforth very different. The Turks also were Mohammedans, but they did not have the same respect for the religion of the Jews and Christians that the Arabs did. Besides, they were fiercer and more bloodthirsty, and in a short time they won from the Eastern Empire lands which the Arabs had never been able to conquer. Even Constantinople was not safe from them.

"From Jerusalem to the Aegean Sea," wrote the Emperor of the East to a Western ruler, "the Turkish hordes have mastered all. Their galleys sweep the Black Sea and the Mediterranean, and threaten the imperial city itself."

In the West, too, quieter times had now come; and rulers and people could turn their attention abroad. Finally, there was now more enthusiasm for religion among all classes; so when pilgrims returned from Jerusalem, telling of outrages committed against Christian persons and against Christian holy places, it was felt to be a shame that this thing should be.

When, therefore, the Emperor of the East wrote to the Pope asking for aid against the Turks, the people of the West were in a mood to grant it. At a great Council held at Clermont, in France, in the year 1095, Pope Urban II. laid the matter before the clergy and princes. Most of those present were French; and Urban, who was himself a Frenchman, spoke to them in their own tongue. He told them of the danger to Constantinople and of the sad state of Jerusalem, while the western peoples were quarreling and fighting among themselves. In all that region, he said, Christians had been led off into slavery, their homes laid waste, and their churches overthrown. Then he appealed to his hearers to remember Charlemagne and the victories which he was believed to have won over the Arabs, and urged them to begin anew the war with the Mohammedans.

"Christ himself," he cried, "will be your leader when you fight for Jerusalem! Let your quarrels cease, and turn your arms against the accursed Turks.

In this way you will return home victorious and laden with the wealth of your foes; or, if you fall in battle, you will receive an everlasting reward!"

With one accord his hearers cried; "It is the will of God! It is the will of God!"

A pilgrim

From all sides they hastened to give in their names for the holy war. Each person promising to go was given a cross of red cloth, which he was to wear upon his breast going to the Holy Land, and on his back returning. To those who "took the cross," the name "Crusaders" was given, from the Latin word which means cross.

The winter following the Council was spent in getting ready. All classes showed the greatest zeal. Preachers went about among the people calling upon rich and poor, noble and peasant alike, to help free the Holy Land; and whole villages, towns, and cities were emptied of their inhabitants to join the Crusade. Many sold all they had to get the means to go; and thieves, robbers, and wicked men of all kinds promised to leave their wickedness and aid in rescuing the tomb of Christ Jesus from the infidels.

The time set for the starting of the Crusade was the early summer of the year 1096. But the common people could not wait so long.

Under a monk named Peter the Hermit, and a poor knight called Walter the Penniless, great companies from Germany and France set out before that time. They had almost no money; they were unorganized; and there was no discipline or obedience in the multitude. The route which they took was down the river Danube, through the kingdoms of the Hungarians and Bulgarians, and so to Constantinople. Few of the people or their leaders had any idea of the distance, and as each new city came in sight many cried out: "Is this Constantinople?"

In Hungary and Bulgaria the people attacked them because they were forced to plunder the country as they passed through, and many were slain. When they reached Constantinople, some of the unruly company set fire to buildings near the city, while others stripped off sheets of lead from the roofs of churches to sell

A crusader

them to Greek merchants. The Emperor hastened to get rid of his unwelcome guests by sending them across into Asia Minor. There within a few months Walter and most of his followers were slain by the Turks; and the expedition came to a sorrowful end.

Meanwhile the princes from France, Germany, and Italy were making ready their expeditions. While the Norman chiefs of Southern Italy were engaged in one of their many wars, a messenger came to them with the news that countless warriors of France had started on the way to Jerusalem, and invited them to join the expedition.

Crusaders on the march

"What are their weapons, what their badge, what their war-cry?" asked one of the Normans.

"Our weapons," replied the messenger, "are those best suited to war; our badge, the cross of Christ; our war-cry, 'It is the will of God! It is the will of God!'"

When he heard these words, the Norman tore from his shoulders his costly cloak, and with his own hands he made crosses from it for all who would follow him to the Holy Land. There he became one of the most famous and renowned of the Crusaders; and his followers showed that they could be as brave, as enterprising, and as skillful in fighting for the Holy Land, as they had been before in fighting for lands and goods in France, in England, and in Italy.

The Crusaders set out at last in five different companies. The first started in August, 1096; the last did not join the others, near Constantinople, until the next summer. The companies were made up of trained and armed knights, with chosen leaders, who had made many preparations for the expedition. They did not suffer so severely, therefore, as did the poor, ignorant people under Walter the Penniless. Still they encountered many hardships. It was already winter when the men of South France toiled over the mountains near Constantinople.

"For three weeks," writes one of their number, "we saw neither bird nor beast. For almost forty days did we struggle on through mists so thick that we could actually feel them and brush them aside with a motion of the hand."

At last this stage of their journey came to an end, and the Crusaders arrived at Constantinople. In the lands north of the Alps, there were at that time none of the vast and richly ornamented churches and other buildings which later arose; all was poor, and lacking in stateliness and beauty. Constantinople, however, was the most beautiful city of the world; so the sight of it filled the Crusaders with awe and admiration.

"Oh how great a city it is!" wrote one of their number; "how noble and beautiful! What wondrously wrought monasteries and palaces are therein! What marvels everywhere in street and square! It would be tedious to recite its wealth in all precious things, in gold and silver, in cloaks of many shapes, and saintly relics. For to this place ships bring all things that man may require."

Now that these sturdy warriors of the West were actually at Constantinople, the Greek Emperor began to fear lest they might prove more troublesome to his empire than the Turks themselves.

"Some of the Crusaders," wrote the Emperor's daughter, "were guileless men and women marching in all simplicity to worship at the tomb of Christ. But there were others of a more wicked kind. Such men had but one object, and this was to get possession of the Emperor's capital."

After much suspicion on both sides, and many disputes, the Emperor got the "Franks"—as the Crusaders were called—safely away from the city, and over into Asia Minor. There, at last, they met the Turks. At first the latter rushed joyously into battle, dragging ropes with which to bind the Christians captive; but soon they found that the "Franks" were more than a match for them. Nicaea, the city where Constantine held the first Church council, was soon taken; and the Crusaders then pressed on to other and greater victories.

Letter-writing was not nearly so common in those days as it is now; but some of the Crusaders wrote letters home, telling of their deeds. A few of these have come down to us across the centuries; and in order that you may learn what the Crusaders were thinking and feeling, as well as what they were doing, one of them is given here. The writer was a rich and powerful noble, and the letter was written while the army was laying siege, with battering rams and siege towers, to the strongly walled city of Antioch.

"Count Stephen to Adele, his sweetest and most amiable wife, to his dear children, and to all his vassals of all ranks,—his greeting and blessing:

"You may be very sure, dearest, that the messenger (whom I send to give you pleasure) left me before Antioch safe and unharmed, and through God's grace in the greatest prosperity. Already at that time we had been continuously advancing for twenty-three weeks toward the home of our Lord Jesus.

You may know for certain, my beloved, that of gold, silver, and many other kinds of riches I now have twice as much as your love had wished for me when I left you. For all our princes, with the common consent of the whole army and against my own wishes, have made me, up to the present time, the leader, chief, and director of their whole expedition.

"You have certainly heard that, after the capture of the city of Nicæa, we fought a great battle with the faithless Turks, and by God's aid conquered them. Next we conquered for the Lord all Roumania, and afterwards Cappadocia. Thence, continually following the wicked Turks, we drove them through the midst of Armenia, as far as the great river Euphrates. Having left all their baggage and beasts of burden on the bank, they fled across the river into Arabia.

"Some of the bolder of the Turkish soldiers, however, entered Syria and hastened by forced marches night and day to enter the royal city of Antioch before our approach. The whole army of God, learning this, gave due praise and thanks to the all-powerful Lord. Hastening with great joy to Antioch, we besieged it, and had many conflicts there with the Turks. Seven times we fought, with the fiercest courage and under the leadership of Christ, against the citizens of Antioch and the innumerable troops which were coming to its aid. In all these seven battles, by the aid of the Lord God, we conquered, and assuredly killed an innumerable host of them. In those battles, indeed, and in very many attacks made upon the city, many of our brethren and followers were killed, and their souls were borne to the joys of Paradise.

"In fighting against these enemies of God and of our own, we have by God's grace endured many sufferings and innumerable evils up to the present time. Many have already exhausted all their resources in this very holy expedition. Very many of our Franks, indeed, would have met death from starvation, if the mercy of God, and our money, had not helped them. Before the city of Antioch, and indeed throughout the whole winter, we suffered for our Lord Christ from excessive cold and great torrents of rain. What some say about the impossibility of bearing the heat of the sun throughout Syria is untrue, for the winter here is very similar to our winter in the West.

"When the Emir of Antioch—that is, its prince and lord—perceived that he was hard pressed by us, he sent his son to the prince who holds Jerusalem, and to the prince of Damascus, and to three other princes. These five Emirs, with 12,000 picked Turkish horsemen, suddenly came to aid the inhabitants of Antioch. We, indeed, ignorant of this, had sent many of our soldiers away to the cities and fortresses; for there are one hundred and sixty-five cities and fortresses throughout Syria which are in our power. But a little before they reached the city, we attacked them at three leagues' distance, with seven hundred soldiers. God surely fought for us against them; for on that day we conquered them and killed an innumerable multitude; and we carried back to the army more than two hundred of their heads, in order that the people might rejoice on that account.

"These things which I write to you are only a few, dearest, of the many deeds which we have done. And because I am not able to tell you, dearest, what is in my mind, I charge you to do right, to carefully watch over your land, to do your duty as you ought to your children and your vassals. You will certainly see me just as soon as I can possibly return to you. Farewell."

The capture of Antioch was the hardest task that the Crusaders had to perform; and it was not until three months later that the city was finally safe in their hands. Many of the Crusaders became discouraged meanwhile and started home.

At this trying time, a priest declared that it had been revealed to him in a dream, thrice repeated, that the head of the spear which had pierced our Lord's side lay buried near one of the altars of a church near by; and it was further revealed, he said, that if this was found and borne at the head of the army, victory would surely follow. After long search, and much prayer and fasting, the "holy lance" was found. Then there was great joy and new courage among the Christians; and when next they marched against the Turks, the Crusaders fought more fiercely than ever.

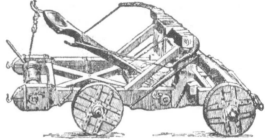

"Thanks to the Lord's Lance," writes one of their number, "none of us were wounded,—no, not so much as by an arrow. I, who speak these things, saw them for myself, since I was bearing the Lord's Lance."

The Crusaders continued to fight valiantly until Antioch was theirs, and the armies which had

Machine for hauling stones

marched to its relief were defeated and scattered.

The Crusaders were now free to march on to Jerusalem. There men and animals suffered much from lack of food and water. "Many," an old writer says, "lay near the dried-up springs unable to utter a cry because of the dryness of their tongues; and there they remained, with open mouths, and hands stretched out to those whom they saw had water."

Again the priests saw visions; and it was promised to the Crusaders that if the army marched barefoot around the city for nine days, the city would fall.

So, a procession was formed, and the Crusaders marched around the city, with white-robed priests and bishops, cross in hand, at their head, chanting hymns and praying as they went. As the procession passed by, the Mohammedans mocked at them from the walls; and some beat a cross, crying out:

"Look, Franks! It is the holy cross on which your Christ was slain!"

After this the chiefs ordered an attack on the city from two sides. The Mohammedans were now beaten back from the walls by the showers of stones thrown by the hurling machines, while blazing arrows carried fire to the roofs of the buildings in the city. Battering rams, too, were at work breaking great holes in the solid walls, and scaling ladders were placed, by which the Christians swarmed over the ramparts. So, at last, the city fell.

Jerusalem,—the holy Jerusalem, which held the tomb of Christ—was now once more in the hands of the Christians. But what a terrible day was that! How little of the meek and just spirit of Christ did his followers show! "When our men had taken the city, with its walls and towers," writes one of the Crusaders, "there were things wondrous to be seen. For some of the enemy—and this is a small matter—were deprived of their heads; others, riddled through with arrows, were forced to leap down from the towers; and others, after long torture, were burned in the flames. In all the streets and squares there were to be seen piles of heads, and hands, and feet; and along the public ways foot and horse alike made passage over the bodies of the slain."

In this way the Crusaders fulfilled their vow to "wrest the Holy Sepulchre from the infidel." How many hundreds of thousands of lives, both Christian and Mohammedan, were lost to gain this end! What agonies of battle, what sufferings on the way, what numbers of women made widows and children left fatherless! And all this that the tomb of Christ might not remain in the hands of a people who did not accept His religion! How pityingly the Christ must have looked down upon this struggle with His mild, sweet eyes! How far away this bloodshed and war seems from the teachings of Him whose birth was heralded by the angels' cry: "Peace on earth, good will towards men!"

"Blessed are the merciful, for they shall obtain mercy," said Christ; but this teaching, alas, the Crusaders seemed not to know.

Later Crusades

After the Holy Land was won, a government had to be organized to prevent the land from slipping back into the hands of the infidels.

The Crusaders knew only one way to rule a land—namely, the feudal way. That was the way Western Europe was ruled, so that was the form of government set up in Palestine. The land was divided into a number of fiefs, and each of these was given to a Crusading chief. In each fief the feudal law and a feudal government was then introduced. Jerusalem, with the country about, was formed into "the Latin Kingdom of Jerusalem," and was given to Godfrey of Bouillon, one of the most famous of the Crusaders. The rest of the land was formed into three principalities, each with its own feudal head, and with many vassal Crusaders.

The peasants who tilled the soil before the Crusaders came were not driven off. They had long been Christians, though they worshiped more like the Greeks than like the Latins. The only difference in their position was that now they were to pay rent and taxes to Christian masters, and not to Turks and Saracens.

As soon as Jerusalem had fallen, most of the Crusaders began to make preparations for returning home. Soon Godfrey and his fellow rulers were left with mere handfuls of men to resist the attacks of the Mohammedans. If the latter had been united, they could easily at this time have driven the "Franks" into the sea. But the Mohammedans were quarreling among themselves, and besides had learned to fear the mail-clad Franks.

So the Christians were given time to prepare their defence. Huge castles were everywhere built to protect the lands they had won. New companies of Crusaders, too, were constantly arriving to take the place of those who had returned home; and merchants from the Italian cities were coming to settle for the purpose of carrying on trade.

Soon, too, three special orders of knights were formed to protect the Holy Land, and care for the Christians. The first of these was the Knights of the Hospital, or the Knights of St. John; its chief purpose was to care for and protect sick pilgrims. The second was the Order of the Temple, or Knights Templar; they got their name because their headquarters were in the temple at Jerusalem. The third was the Order of the Teutonic Knights, which received its name because its members were Germans, while the members of the other orders were mostly French.

Knights Templar

The members of these orders were both monks and knights. They were bound like monks by vows of poverty, chastity, and obedience; but they were also knights engaged in a perpetual crusade against the infidel. The Hospitallers wore a white cross on a black mantle; the Templars a red cross on a white mantle; and the Teutonic Knights a black cross on a mantle of white. These "military orders" became very powerful and wealthy, and helped a great deal to keep the Holy Land in the hands of the Christians.

For nearly half a century after Jerusalem was recovered there was no very great danger to the rule of the Franks. Then all Europe was startled by the news that one of the four Christian principalities had been conquered by the Saracens, and the Christians put to the sword. At once there was great fear lest the other states should fall also, and preparations were made for sending out a large number of Crusaders to their assistance.

This expedition started in the year 1147, and is known as the Second Crusade. The kings of two of the leading countries of Europe, Conrad III. of Germany and Louis VII. of France, led the forces. Their armies took the same route—down the river Danube and across to Constantinople—that the first Crusade had followed. Again there was terrible suffering on the way. The German army was almost entirely destroyed in Asia Minor; and although the French reached Palestine in safety, very little was accomplished in the way of strengthening the Christians there.

After the failure of this Crusade, there was no great change for forty years. Twice a year, in the spring and autumn, a number of vessels would sail from the cities of Italy and Southern France carrying pilgrims and adventurers to Palestine. In this way the strength of the Christian states was kept up, in spite of the number who were constantly returning.

Towards the end of this period, rumors began to come of a great Mohammedan leader who had arisen in Egypt, and was threatening Palestine with new danger. He was called Saladin, and was one of the greatest rulers the Mohammedans ever had. He was foremost in battle, and wise and far-sighted in council. When he was victorious, he dealt generously with his enemies; and when defeated he was never cast down. He was ever simple in his habits, just and upright in his dealings, and true to his promises. He was, in short, as chivalrous a warrior, and as sincere a believer in his faith, as any of the Christian knights against whom he fought.

For Saladin, as well as for the Crusaders, the war for Palestine was a "holy war"; and soon his power was grown so great that he could attack them from all sides.

"So great is the multitude of the Saracens and Turks," wrote one of the Crusaders in speaking of his armies, "that from the city of Tyre, which they are besieging, they cover the face of the earth as far as Jerusalem, like an innumerable army of ants."

When the Christians marched out to battle, they were overthrown with terrible slaughter; and the King of Jerusalem, and the Grand Master of the Templars, were among the captives taken. Three months after this, Saladin laid siege to Jerusalem itself. For two weeks only the city held out; at the end of that time it was forced to sue for peace.

The mercy which Saladin now showed to the conquered Christians was in strange contrast to the cruelty which the Crusaders had displayed when the city fell into their hands. There was no slaughter such as had occurred ninety years before, and the greater number of the defeated party were allowed to go free, on paying a ransom. But the crosses on the churches were torn down, the bells were destroyed, and the churches themselves were changed into Mohammedan mosques. Once more the Holy Land was in the hands of the unbelievers.

When news of these events reached Europe, it caused great excitement. The three most powerful rulers,—Frederick of Germany, Philip of France, and Richard the Lion-Hearted of England,—took the cross, and in the years 1189 and 1190 they led forth their followers to the Third Crusade.

The Emperor Frederick of Germany,—who was called "Barbarossa," on account of his red beard,—had been one of those who followed King Conrad in the Second Crusade; now although he was seventy years old, he was the first to start on the Third. He led his army by the old land route, but his forces were better organized, and there was not so much hardship as there had been before. Except for one battle which they had to fight with the Greek Emperor, all went well until the army reached Asia Minor. There, alas! The old Emperor was drowned, while swimming a river one hot day, to refresh himself and shorten his way. After that the German army went to pieces, and most of its members lost their lives in the mountains and deserts of Asia Minor, or were cut down by Turkish soldiers.

The legend of Barbarossa

In Germany the people refused to believe that their king was dead. Long after this, stories were told of the good Barbarossa, who slept from year to year in a rocky cavern high up on a lonely mountain side, with his head resting on his hand and his long red beard grown round the granite blocks by his side. There, the people said, he lay sleeping throughout the ages; but when the ravens should cease to fly about the mountain, the Emperor would wake to punish the wicked and bring back the golden age to the world.

When at last Philip of France and Richard of England were ready, they took ship to avoid the hardships of the journey by land. From the beginning, however, things went wrong. Richard and Philip were very jealous of each other, and could not get along together. Philip was only half-hearted in the Crusade, and longed to be back in France; while Richard allowed himself to be turned aside for a while to other things.

When they reached the Holy Land, they found the Christians laying siege to Acre, one of the sea-ports near Jerusalem. The siege had already lasted more than a year, and for several months longer it dragged on. It was a dreary time for the Christians. "The Lord is not in the camp," wrote one of their number; "there is none that doeth good. The leaders strive with one another, while the lesser folk starve, and have none to help. The Turks are persistent in attack, while our

Attacking a city

knights skulk within their tents. The strength of Saladin increases daily, but daily does our army wither away."

At last Acre was taken,—mainly through the skill and daring of King Richard, who was one of the best warriors of that day, and knew well how to use the battering-rams, stone-throwers, moveable towers, and other military "engines" to batter down walls and take cities. Philip was already weary of the Crusade, and soon after returned to France. Richard remained for more than a year longer. In this time he won some military successes; but he could not take Jerusalem.

Finally news came to Richard from England that his brother John was plotting to make himself king. Richard was now obliged to return home. The only

76

advantage he had gained for the Christians was a truce for three years, permitting pilgrims to go to the Holy Sepulchre at Jerusalem without hindrance.

Before he left, Richard warned Saladin that he would return to renew the war; but he never did. On his way home he was shipwrecked and was obliged to pass by land through Germany. There he was recognized by his enemies, and kept prisoner till he paid a heavy ransom. Then, after his release, he found himself engaged in troubles with his brother John, and in war with King Philip; and at last, in the year 1199, he died from an arrow wound while fighting in France.

Movable tower

The remaining Crusades are not of so much importance as the First and the Third.

On the Fourth Crusade, the Crusaders were persuaded by the Venetians to attack the Christian city of Constantinople. In this way the Greek Empire passed for fifty years into the hands of the Latin Christians. The Venetians were the ones who chiefly profited by this Crusade, for they secured many islands in the Eastern Mediterranean Sea, and important trading privileges.

As a result of the Fifth Crusade, Jerusalem was recovered for a while; but this was accomplished through a treaty, and not as the result of victories won by arms.

The Sixth Crusade was led by the good king, St. Louis of France. The Crusaders now sought to attack the Saracens in Egypt; but they were defeated, and the French king himself was captured and forced to pay a heavy ransom to secure his freedom.

The last Crusade was the Seventh, which was also led by St. Louis of France. Now the Crusaders attacked the Saracens in Tunis. Again the Crusade was a failure, and this time the French king lost his life, through a sickness which broke out in the army.

After this, for more than a century, popes and kings talked of crusades, and raised taxes and made preparations for them. But though they fought the heathen in Prussia, and the Mohammedans in Spain and in Hungary, no more crusades went to the Holy Land to win the sepulchre of Christ from the infi-del. Men no longer thought that this was so important as it had once seemed to them; and no doubt they were right. It doesn't make so much difference who rules the land where Christ lived and died; the great question is whether Christ lives and rules in the hearts and lives of those who follow Him.

Although the Crusades failed in what they were intended to accomplish, they had some very important results. The returning Crusaders broguht back with them many plants and other things which were new to Europe. Among these were the sugar cane, orange, lemon, watermelon, apricot, and rice. Cot-tons, muslins, damask, satin, velvet, and new dye-stuffs were also introduced. Besides these new products, there were changes at home which were even more important. The expense of setting forth on the Crusades caused many lords to free their serfs in return for money, and to sell to the towns which were on their lands the right to govern themselves. The power of the nobles was thus weakened by these expeditions, while that of the King and towns was strengthened.

Most important of all was the influence of the Crusades on ideas. For near-ly two hundred years men were going and coming in great number to and from the Holy Land, seeing strange countries and strange peoples, and learn-ing new customs. Before the Crusades, each district lived by itself, and its inhabitants scarcely ever heard of the rest of the world. During the Crusades this separation was broken down, and people from all parts of Christendom met together. In this way men came to learn more of the world, and of the people who dwelt in it; and their minds were broadened by this knowledge. Never after the Crusades, as a result, was the life of man quite so dark, so dreary, and so narrow, as it had been before. From this time on, the Middle Ages gradually changed their character; for influences were now at work to bring this period to an end, and bring about the beginning of Modern Times.

Life of the Castle

Before we consider what the influences were which brought the Middle Ages to a close, we must see more clearly what the life of that period was like. We will first read about the life of the castle, where lordly knights and gentle ladies dwelt. Then we will see what was the manner of life of the peasants who dwelt in the villages, and the merchants and craftsmen who dwelt in the cities and towns. Finally we will visit the monasteries, and see what was the life of the monks and nuns, who gave their lives to the service and praise of God.

If you visit France, Germany, and other European countries to-day, you will find everywhere the ruins of massive stone castles, rearing their tall towers on the hilltops, and commanding the passage of roads and rivers. At the pre-sent time these are mostly tumbled down, and overgrown with moss and ivy, and nobody cares to live within their dark walls.

A castle of the eleventh century

In the Middle Ages it was not so. Then they were the safest places in which to live; so in spite of their cold and gloom, they became the centers of the life of the time. It was from the castles that the feudal barons ruled their lands. It was there that the people found refuge from the attacks of the Northmen and Hungarians. It was from the castles that the Crusaders set out for the Holy Land. In them chivalry was born and flourished; at their gates tournaments, jousts, and other knightly festivals took place; and in their halls the wandering singers, who were building up a new literature, found the readiest welcome and the most eager and appreciative listeners.

Let us fancy ourselves back in the eleventh or twelfth century, and examine a castle. We shall find the country very different, we may be sure, from what it is to-day. Great thick forests stand where now there are flourishing towns; and everything has a wilder, more unsettled look.

Here is a castle, in France, that will suit our purpose. It was built by one of the vassals of William the Conqueror, and has been the scene of many sieges and battles. See how everything is arranged so as to make easy its defence. It is built on the top of a steep hill; and around its walls a deep ditch or moat is dug. At the outer edge of the moat we see a strong fence or palisade of heavy stakes set in the ground. Just inside this is a path, along which the sentries march in time of war. The gate, too, is doubly and triply guarded. In front of it is a drawbridge across the moat—indeed, there are two; and the space between is guarded by a protecting wall. In later days these drawbridges were made stronger and more complicated, and heavy towers with walls of masonry were built, the better to protect the entrance.

When we have passed these outer works, we come to a heavy wooden door between two tall towers which mark the entrance to the walls. We pass through this, and find ourselves within the gateway. But we are still far from being in the castle. In the narrow vaulted passage-way before us, we see suspended a heavy iron grating, called the portcullis, which may come rattling down at any moment to bar our passage. And beyond this is another door; and beyond this another portcullis. The entrance to the castle is indeed well guarded; and the porter who keeps watch at the gate, and has to open and shut all these barriers, is at times a busy man.

At last we are past the gateway and find ourselves in an open courtyard. The thick walls of the castle surround us on all sides, and at their top we see the battlements and loopholes through which arrows may be shot at the enemy. Here and there the wall is protected by stone towers, in which are stairways leading to the battlements above. In the first courtyard we find the stables, where the lord of the castle keeps his horses. Here, too, is space for the shelter of the villagers in time of war; and here, perhaps, is the great brick oven in which bread is baked to feed the lord and all his followers.

Going on we come to a wall or palisade, which separates the courtyard we are in from one lying beyond it. In later times this wall, too, was made much stronger than we find it here. Passing through a gateway, we come into the second courtyard. Here again we find a number of buildings, used for different purposes. In one are the storerooms and cellars, where provisions are kept to enable the dwellers in the castle to stand a siege. Next to this is a building shaped like a great jug, with a large chimney at the top, and smaller ones in a circle round about. This is the kitchen, in which the food is cooked for the lord of the castle and his household. The cooking, we may be sure, is usually simple,—most of the meats being roasted on spits over open fires, and elaborate dishes, with sauces and spices, being unknown. Most castles have, in addition, a small church or chapel in this courtyard, in which the inhabitants may worship.

The most important building of all is still to be described. There at the end of the courtyard we see the tall "keep" of the castle, which the French called "donjon," and in whose basement there are "dungeons" indeed, for traitors and captured enemies. This is the true stronghold of the baron, and it is a secure retreat. Think of all the hard fighting there must be before the enemy can even reach it. The drawbridges must be crossed, the gates must be battered down, and the portcullises pried up; the first courtyard must be cleared; the dividing wall must be carried; the second courtyard also must be cleared of its defenders. And when the enemy, bruised and worn, at last arrive at the keep, their work is just begun. There the lord and his followers will make their last stand, and the fighting will be fiercer than ever.

The walls of the keep are of stone, eight to ten feet thick; and from the loopholes in its frowning sides peer skilled archers and crossbowmen, ready to let fly their bolts and arrows at all in sight. A long, long siege will be necessary, to starve out its defenders. If this is not done, movable towers must be erected, battering rams placed, stone-hurling machines brought up, blazing arrows shot at the roof and windows, and tunnels dug to undermine the walls. In this way the castle may be burned, or an entrance at last be gained. But even then there will be fierce fighting in the narrow passageways, in the dimly-lighted halls, and on the winding stairways which lead from story to story. It will be long, indeed, before our lord's banner is torn from the summit of the tower, and his enemy's is placed in its stead! And even when all is lost, there still remain hidden stairways in the castle walls, underground passages opening into the moat, and the gate in the rear, through which the lord and his garrison may yet escape to the woods and open fields; and so continue the battle another day.

In later days, stronger and more complicated castles were erected, especially after Western lords had begun to go on the Crusades, and had seen the great fortresses of the Eastern Empire. The picture on the following page shows such a castle, erected in Normandy by Richard the Lion-Hearted, and called by him the "Saucy Castle" *(Chateau Gaillard)* because of its defiance of the French King. The picture also shows hurling engines set for attack, and a movable tower being brought to scale its walls.

But let us inquire rather concerning the life of the castle in time of peace. Where and how does the lord and his household live? How are his children educated? And with what do they amuse themselves in the long days when there is no enemy to attack their walls, and no distant expedition in which to engage?

Sometimes the lord and his family live in the upper stories of the huge donjon, where arms and supplies are always stored. But this is so gloomy, with its thick walls and narrow windows, that many lords build more comfortable "halls" in their courtyards, and prefer to live in these.

Let us look in upon such a "hall," whether it is in the donjon, or in a separate building. There we find a great wide room, large enough to hold all the inhabitants of the castle, when the lord wishes to gather them about him. This is the real center of the life of the castle. Here the lord eats and sleeps; here the great banquets are given; here he receives his vassals to do homage; here he plays chess and backgammon with his companions; and here in the evening the inmates gather, perchance to listen to the songs and tales of wandering minstrels.

Within the castle are many people, occupying themselves in many ways. In the courtyards are servants and dependents caring for the horses, cooking in the kitchen, and busily engaged in other occupations. Elsewhere are those whose duty it is to guard the castle—the porter at the gate, the watchman on the tower, and the men-at-arms to defend the walls in case of attack. Besides these we see many boys and young men who are evidently of too noble birth to be servants, and yet are too young to be warriors. Who can they be?

These are the sons of the lord of the castle, and of other lords, who are learning to be knights. Their training is long and careful. Until he is seven years old, the little noble is left to the care of his mother and the women of the castle. At the age of seven his knightly education begins. Usually the boy is sent away from home to the castle of his father's lord, or some famous knight, there to be brought up and trained for knighthood.

From the age of seven till he reaches the age of fourteen, the boy is called a page or "varlet," which means "little vassal." There he waits upon the lord and lady of the castle. He serves them at table, and he attends to them when they ride forth to the chase. From them he learns lessons of honor and bravery, of love and chivalry. Above all, he learns how to ride and handle a horse.

When the young noble has become a well-grown lad of fourteen or fifteen, he is made a "squire." Now it is his duty to look after his lord's horses and arms. The horses must be carefully groomed every morning, and the squire must see that their shoes are all right. He must also see that his lord's arms and armor are kept bright and free from rust. When the lord goes forth to war, his squire accompanies him, riding on a big strong horse, and carrying his lord's shield and lance. When the lord goes into battle, his squire must stay near, leading a spare steed and ready to hand his master fresh weapons at any moment. After several years of this service, the squire may himself be allowed to use weapons and fight at his lord's side; and sometimes he may even be allowed to ride forth alone in search of adventures.

In this manner the squire learns the business of a knight, which is fighting. But he also learns his amusements and accomplishments.

Let us approach a group of squires in the castle hall, when their work is done, and they are tired of chess and backgammon. They are discussing, perhaps, as to which is the more interesting, hunting or falconry; and we may hear a delicate featured squire hold forth in this way:

"What can be prettier than a bright-eyed, well- trained falcon hawk? And what can be pleasanter than the sport of flying it at the birds? Take some fine September morning, when the sky is blue and the air is fresh, and our lord and lady ride forth with their attendants. Each carries his falcon on his gloved left hand, and we hurry forward in pursuit of cranes, herons, ducks, and other

A lady hawking

birds. When one is sighted, a falcon is unhooded, and let fly at it. The falcon's bells tinkle merrily as it rises. Soon it is in the air above the game, and swift as an arrow it darts upon the prey, plunging its talons into it, and crouching over it until the hunter gallops up to recover both falcon and prey. This is the finest hunting. And what skill is necessary, too, in rearing and training the birds! Ah, falconry is the sport for me!"

But this does not seem to be the opinion of most of the group. Their views are expressed by a tall, strongly-built squire, who says:

"Falconry is all right for women and boys, but it is not the sport for men. What are your falcons to my hounds and harriers! The education of one good boar-hound, I can tell you, requires as much care as all your falcons; and when you are done the dog loves you, and that is more than you can say for your hawks. And the chase itself is far more exciting. The hounds are uncoupled, and set yelping upon the scent, and away we dash after them, plunging through the woods, leaping glades and streams in our haste. At last we reach the spot where the game has turned at bay, and find an enormous boar, defending himself stoutly and fiercely against the hounds. Right and left he rolls the dogs. With his back bristling with rage, he charges straight for the huntsmen. Look out, now; for his sharp tusks cut like a knife! But the huntsmen are skilled, and the dogs play well their part. Before the beast can reach man or horse, he is pierced by a dozen spears, and is nailed to the ground, dead! Isn't this a nobler sport than hawking?"

Arming the knight

So, we may be sure, most of the knights and squires will agree. But the ladies, and many of the squires and knights, will still love best the sport of falconry.

In this way the squire spends his days until he reaches the age of twenty or twenty-one. He has now proved both his courage and his skill, and at last his lord says that he has "earned his spurs."

A great feast in the twelfth century

So the squire is to be made a knight; and this is the occasion for great festivities. In company with other squires who are candidates for knighthood, he must go through a careful preparation. First comes the bath, which is the mark of purification. Then he puts on garments of red, white, and black. The red means the blood he is willing to shed in defence of the Church and of the oppressed; the white means that his mind is pure and clean; and the black is to remind him of death, which comes to all.

Next comes the "watching of the arms." All night the squires keep watch, fasting and praying, before the altar in the church on which their arms have been placed; and though they may stand or kneel, they must on no account sit or lie down. At the break of day the priest comes. After they have each confessed their sins to him, they hear mass and take the holy sacrament. Perhaps, too, the priest preaches a sermon on the proud duties of a knight, and the obligations which they owe to God and the Church.

At last the squires assemble in the courtyard of the castle, or in some open place outside the walls. There they find great numbers of knights and ladies who have come to grace the occasion of their knighting. Each squire in turn now takes his place on a carpet which is spread on the ground, and his friends and relatives assist in girding on his armor and his sword. Then comes the most trying moment of all. His father or his lord advances and gives him what is called the "accolade." At first this was a heavy blow with the fist, given upon the squire's neck; but later it was with the flat of a sword upon his shoulder. At the same time the person who gives the accolade cries out:

"In the name of God, and St. Michael, and St. George, I dub thee knight! Be brave and loyal!"

The squire is now a knight, but the festival is not yet over. The new-made knights must first give an exhibition of their skill in riding and handling their horses, and in striking with their lances marks which are set up for them to ride at. Then comes fencing with their swords on horseback. Perhaps this is followed by a regular "tournament," in which knights, both old and new, ride against one another in mimic warfare. With closed helmets and lowered lances, the knights charge at one another, each seeking to unhorse his opponent. Lances are shattered, armor battered, and sometimes serious wounds are received in this rough sport; while bright-eyed ladies sit beside the "lists," to inspire their knights to brave deeds in their honor. Then the day is wound up with a great feast, and music and the distribution of presents.

At last, the guests depart; and the new-made knights go off to bed, to dream of Saracens to be fought in the Holy Land, and dragons to be slain, and wicked knights to be encountered,—and above all, of beautiful maidens to be rescued and served with loyalty and love.

So they dream the dreams of chivalry. And when they awaken, the better ones among them—but not all, alas!—will seek to put their dreams into action.

Life of the Village

One thing about the life of the knights and squires has not yet been explained; that is, how they were supported. They neither cultivated the fields, nor manufactured articles for sale, nor engaged in commerce. How, then, were they fed and clothed, and furnished with their expensive armor and horses? How, in short, was all this life of the castle kept up,—with its great buildings, its constant wars, its costly festivals, and its idleness?

We may find the explanation of this in the saying of a bishop who lived in the early part of the Middle Ages.

"God," said he, "divided the human race from the beginning into three classes. There were, the priests, whose duty it was to pray and serve God; the knights, whose duty is was to defend society; and the peasants, whose duty it was to till the soil and support by their labor the other classes."

This, indeed, was the arrangement as it existed during the whole of the Middle Ages. The "serfs" and "villains" who tilled the soil, together with the merchants and craftsmen of the towns, bore all the burden of supporting the more picturesque classes above them.

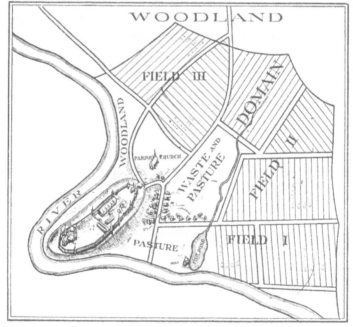

Plan of a village

The peasants were called "serfs" and "villains," and their position was very curious. For several miles about the castle, all the land belonged to its lord, and was called, in England, his "manor." He did not own the land outright,—for, as you know, he did homage and fealty for it to *his* lord or "suzerain," and the latter in turn owed homage and fealty to *his* "suzerain," and so on up to the king. Neither did the lord of the castle keep all of the manor lands in his own hands. He did not wish to till the land himself, so most of it was divided up and tilled by peasants, who kept their shares as long as they lived, and passed them on to their children after them. As long as the peasants performed the services and made the payments which they owed to the lord, the latter could not rightfully turn them out of their land.

The part of the manor which the lord kept in his own hands was called his "domain," and we shall see presently how this was used. In addition there were certain parts which were used by the peasants as common pastures for their cattle and sheep; that is, they all had joint rights in this. Then there was the woodland to which the peasants might each send a certain number of pigs to feed upon the beech nuts and acorns. Finally there was the part of the manor which was given over to the peasants to till.

This was usually divided into three great fields, without any fences, walls, or hedges about them. In one of these we should find wheat growing, or some other grain that is sown in the winter; in another we should find a crop of some grain, such as oats, which requires to be sown in the spring; while in the third we should find no crop at all. The next year the arrangement would be changed, and again the next year. In this way, each field bore winter grain one year, spring grain the next, and the third year it was plowed several times and allowed to rest to recover its fertility. While resting it was said to "lie fallow." Then the round was repeated. This whole arrangement was due to the fact that people in those days did not know as much about "fertilizers" and "rotation of crops" as we do now.

The most curious arrangement of all was the way the cultivated land was divided up. Each peasant had from ten to forty acres of land which he cultivated; and part of this lay in each of the three fields. But instead of lying all together, it was scattered about in long narrow strips, each containing about an acre, with strips of unplowed sod separating the plowed strips from one another. This was a very unsatisfactory arrangement, because each peasant had to waste so much time in going from one strip to his next; and nobody has ever been able to explain quite clearly how it ever came about. But this is the arrangement which prevailed in almost all civilized countries throughout the whole of the Middle Ages, and indeed in some places for long afterward.

Plowing

In return for the land which the peasant held from his lord, he owed the latter many payments and many services. He paid fixed sums of money at different times during the year; and if his lord or his lord's suzerain knighted his eldest son, or married off his eldest daughter, or went on a crusade, or was taken captive and had to be ransomed,—then the peasant must pay an additional sum. At Easter and at other fixed times the peasant brought a gift of eggs or chickens to his lord; and he also gave the lord one or more of his lambs and pigs each year for the use of the pasture. At harvest time the lord received a portion of the grain raised on the peasant's land. In addition the peasant must grind his grain at his lord's mill, and pay the charge for this; he must also bake his bread in the great oven which belonged to the lord, and use his lord's presses in making his cider and wine, paying for each.

These *payments* were sometimes burdensome enough, but they were not nearly so burdensome as the *services* which the peasants owed their lord. All the labor of cultivating the lord's "domain" land was performed by them. They plowed it with their great clumsy plows and ox-teams; they harrowed it, and sowed it, and weeded it, and reaped it; and finally they carted the sheaves to the lord's barns and threshed them by beating with great jointed clubs or "flails." And when the work was done, the grain belonged entirely to the lord. About two days a week were spent this way in working on the lord's domain; and the peasants could only work on their own lands between times. In addition, if the lord decided to build new towers, or a new gate, or to erect new buildings in the castle, the peasants had to carry stone and mortar for the building and help the paid masons in every way possible.

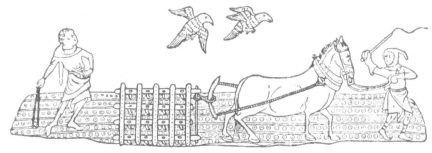

Harrowing

And when the demands of their lord were satisfied, there were still other demands made upon them; for every tenth sheaf of grain, and every tenth egg, lamb and chicken, had to be given to the Church as "tithes."

The peasants did not live scattered about the country as our farmers do, but dwelt all together in an open village. If we should take our stand there on a day in spring, we should see much to interest us. On the hilltop above is the lord's castle; and near by is the parish church with the priest's house. In the distance are the green fields, cut into long narrow strips; and in them we see men plowing and harrowing with teams of slow-moving oxen, while women are busy with hooks and tongs weeding the growing grain. Close at hand in the village we hear the clang of the blacksmith's anvil, and the miller's song as he carries the sacks of grain and flour to and from the mill. Dogs are barking, donkeys are braying, cattle are lowing; and through it all we hear the sound of little children at play or women singing at their work.

Threshing with flails

The houses themselves were often little better than wooden huts thatched with straw or rushes, though sometimes they were of stone. Even at the best they were dark, dingy, and unhealthful. Chimneys were just beginning to be used in the Middle Ages for the castles of the great lords; but in the peasants' houses the smoke was usually allowed to escape through the doorway. The door was often made so that the upper half could be left open for this purpose, while the lower half was closed. The cattle were usually housed under the same roof with the peasant's family; and in some parts of Europe this practice is still followed.

Within the houses we should not find very much furniture. Here is a list of the things which one family owned in the year 1345:

> 2 feather beds, 15 linen sheets, and 4 striped yellow counterpanes.
>
> 1 hand-mill for grinding meal, a pestle and mortar for pounding grain, 2 grain chests, a kneading trough, and 2 ovens over which coals could be heaped for baking.
>
> 2 iron tripods on which to hang kettles over the fire; 2 metal pots and 1 large kettle.
>
> 1 metal bowl, 2 brass water jugs, 4 bottles, a copper box, a tin washtub, a metal warming-pan, 2 large chests, a box, a cupboard, 4 tables on trestles, a large table, and a bench.
>
> 2 axes, 4 lances, a crossbow, a scythe, and some other tools.

The food and clothing of the peasant were coarse and simple, but were usually sufficient for his needs. At times, however, war or a succession of bad seasons would bring famine upon a district. Then the suffering would be terrible; for there were no provisions saved up, and the roads were so bad and communication so difficult that it was hard to bring supplies from other regions where there was plenty. At such times, the peasants suffered most. They were forced to eat roots, herbs, and the bark of trees; and often they died by hundreds for want of even such food.

Thus you will see that the lot of the peasant was a hard one; and it was often made still harder by the cruel contempt which the nobles felt for those whom they looked upon as "base-born." The name "villains" was given the peasants because they lived in villages; but the nobles have handed down the name as a term of reproach. In a poem, which was written to please the nobles no doubt, the writer scolds at the villain because he was too well fed, and, as he says, "made faces" at the clergy. "Ought he to eat fish?" the poet asks. "Let him eat thistles, briars, thorns, and straw, on Sunday, for fodder; and pea-husks during the week! Let him keep watch all his days, and have trouble. Thus ought villains to live. Ought he to eat meats? He ought to go naked on all fours, and crop herbs with the horned cattle in the fields!"

Of course there were many lords who did not feel this way towards their peasants. Ordinarily the peasant was not nearly so badly off as the slave in the Greek and Roman days; and often, perhaps, he was as well off as many of the peasants of Europe to-day. But there was this difference between his position and that of the peasant now. Many of them could not leave their lord's manors and move elsewhere without their lord's permission. If they did so, their lord could pursue them and bring them back; but if they succeeded in getting to a free town, and dwelt there for a year and a day without being recaptured, then they became freed from their lord, and might dwell where they chose.

Life of the Town

We must now consider the life of the towns during the Middle Ages.

The Germans had never lived in cities in their old homes; so when they came into the Roman Empire they preferred the free life of the country to settling within the town walls. The old Roman cities which had sprung up all over the Empire had already lost much of their importance; and under these country-loving conquerors they soon lost what was left. In many places the inhabitants entirely disappeared; other places decreased in size; and all lost the right which they had had of governing themselves.

The inhabitants of the towns became no better off than the peasants who lived in the little villages. In both the people lived by tilling the soil. In both the lord of the district made laws, appointed officers, and settled disputes in his own court. There was little difference indeed between the villages and towns, except a difference in size.

This was the condition of things during the early part of the Middle Ages, while feudalism was slowly arising, and the nobles were beating back the attacks of the Saracens, the Hungarians, and the Northmen.

At last, in the tenth and eleventh centuries, as we have seen, this danger was overcome. Now men might travel from place to place without constant danger of being robbed or slain. Commerce and manufacturers began to spring up again, and the people of the towns supported themselves by these as well as by agriculture. With commerce and manufactures, too, came riches. This was especially true in Italy and Southern France, where the townsmen were able by their position to take part in the trade with Constantinople and Egypt, and also to gain money by carrying pilgrims and Crusaders in their ships to the Holy Land. With riches, too, came power; and with power came the desire to free themselves from the rule of their lord.

So, all over civilized Europe, during the eleventh, twelfth, and thirteenth centuries, we find new towns arising, and old ones getting the right to govern themselves.

In Italy the towns gained power first; then in Southern France; then in Northern France; and then along the valley of the river Rhine, and the coasts of the Baltic Sea. Sometimes the towns bought their freedom from their lords; sometimes they won it after long struggles and much fighting. Sometimes the nobles and clergy were wise enough to join with the townsmen, and share in the benefits which the town brought; sometimes they fought them foolishly and bitterly.

In Germany and in Italy the power of the kings was not great enough to make much difference one way or the other. In France the kings favored the towns against their lords, and used them to break down the power of the feudal nobles. Then, when the king's power had become so strong that they no longer feared the nobles, they checked the power of the towns lest they in turn might become powerful and independent.

Thus, in different ways and at different times, there grew up the cities of mediaeval Europe.

In Italy there sprang up the free cities of Venice, Florence, Pisa, Genoa, and others, where scholars and artists were to arise and bring a new birth to learning and art; where, also, daring seamen were to be trained, like Columbus, Cabot, and Vespucius, to discover, in later times, the New World. In France the citizens showed their skill by building those beautiful Gothic cathedrals which are still so much admired. In the towns of Germany and Holland clever workmen invented and developed the art of printing, and so made possible the learning and education of to-day.

The civilization of modern times, indeed, owes a great debt to these old towns and their sturdy inhabitants.

Let us see now what those privileges were which the townsmen got, and which enabled them to help on the world's progress so much. To us these privileges would not seem so very great. In hundreds of towns in France the lords granted only such rights as the following:

1. The townsmen shall pay only small fixed sums for the rent of their lands, and as a tax when they sell goods, etc.

2. They shall not be obliged to go to war for their lord, unless they can return the same day if they choose.

3. When they have law-suits, the townsmen shall not be obliged to go outside the town to have them tried.

4. No charge shall be made for the use of the town oven; and the townsmen may gather the dead wood in the lord's forest for fuel.

5. The townsmen shall be allowed to sell their property when they wish, and leave the town without hindrance from the lord.

6. Any peasant who remains a year and a day in the town, without being claimed by his lord, shall be free.

In other places the townsmen got in addition the right to elect their own judges; and in still others they got the right to elect *all* their officers.

Towns of this latter class were sometimes called "communes." Over them the lord had very little right, except to receive such sums of money as it was agreed should be paid to him. In some places, as in Italy, these communes became practically independent, and had as much power as the lords themselves. They made laws, and coined money, and had their vassals, and waged war just as the lords did. But there was this important difference: in the communes the rights belonged to *the citizens as a whole*, and not to one person. This made all the citizens feel an interest in the town affairs, and produced an enterprising, determined spirit among them. At the same time, the citizens were trained in the art of self-government in using these rights. In this way the world was being prepared for a time when governments like ours,—"of the people, for the people, and by the people,"—should be possible.

But this was to come only after many, many years. The townsmen often used their power selfishly, and in the interest of their families and their own class. Often the rich and powerful townsmen were as cruel and harsh toward the poorer and weaker classes as the feudal lords themselves. Fierce and bitter struggles often broke out in the towns, between the citizens who had power, and those who had none. Often, too, there were great family quarrels, continued from generation to generation, like the one which is told of in Shakespeare's play, "Romeo and Juliet."

In Italy there came in time to be two great parties called the "Guelfs" and the "Ghibellines." At first there was a real difference in views between them; but by and by they became merely two rival factions. Then Guelfs were known from Ghibellines by the way they cut their fruit at table; by the color of roses they wore; by the way they yawned, and spoke, and were clad. Often the struggles and brawls became so fierce in a city that to get a little peace the townsmen would call in an outsider to rule over them for a while.

With the citizens so divided among themselves, it will not surprise you to learn that the communes everywhere at last lost their independence. They passed under the rule of the king, as in France; or else, as happened in Italy, they fell into the power of some "tyrant" or local lord.

But let us think, not of the weaknesses and mistakes of these old townsmen, but of their earnest, busy life, and its quaint surroundings. Imagine yourself a peasant lad, fleeing from your lord or coming for the first time to the market in a mediaeval town.

As we approach the city gates we see that the walls are strong and crowned with turrets; and the gate is defended with drawbridge and portcullis like the entrance to a castle. Within, are narrow, winding streets, with rows of tall-roofed houses, each with its garden attached. The houses themselves are more like our houses to-day than like the Greek and Roman ones; for they have no courtyard in the

Cathedral of Cologne

interior and are several stories high. The roadway is unpaved, and full of mud; and there are no sewers. If you walk the streets after nightfall, you must carry a torch to light your footsteps, for there are no street-lamps. There are no policemen; but if you are out after dark, you must beware the "city watch," who take turns in guarding the city, for they will make you give a strict account of yourself.

Now, however, it is day, and we need have no fear. Presently we come into the business parts of the city, and there we find the different trades grouped together in different streets. Here are the goldsmiths, and there are the tanners; here the cloth merchants, and there the butchers; here the armor-smiths, and there the money-changers. The shops are all small and on the ground floor, with their wares exposed for sale in the open windows.

Let us look in at one of the goldsmiths' shops. The shop-keeper and his wife are busily engaged waiting on customers and inviting passers-by to stop and examine their goods. Within we see several men and boys at work, making the goods which their master sells. There the gold is melted and refined; the right amount of alloy is mixed with it; then it is cast, beaten, and filed into the proper shape. Then perhaps the article is enameled and jewels are set in it.

All of these things are done in this one little shop; and so it is for each trade. The workmen must all begin at the beginning, and start with the rough material; and the "apprentices," as the boys are called, must learn each of the

A Medieval shop

processes by which the raw material is turned into the finished article.

Thus a long term of apprenticeship is necessary for each trade, lasting sometimes for ten years. During this time the boys are fed, clothed and lodged with their master's family above the shop, and receive no pay. If they misbehave, he has the right to punish them; and if they run away, he can pursue them and bring them back. Their life, however, is not so hard as that of the peasant boys, for they are better fed and housed, and have more to look forward to.

When their apprenticeship is finished, they will become full members of the "guild" of their trade, and may work for whatever master they please. For a while they may wander from city to city, working now for this master and now for that. In each city they will find the workers at their trade all united together into a guild, with a charter from the king or other lord which permits them to make rules for carrying on of that business and to shut out all persons from it who have not served a regular apprenticeship. So, in each important town there were "craft guilds" of stone-cutters, plasterers, carpenters, blacksmiths, weavers, and the like, as well as a "merchant guild," composed of those who traded to other places.

The more ambitious boys will not be content with a mere workman's life. They will look forward to a time when they shall have saved up money enough to start in business for themselves. Then they too will become masters, with workmen and apprentices under them; and perhaps, in course of time, if they grow in wealth and wisdom, they may be elected rulers over the city.

A fair in the thirteenth century

Let us leave the shops of the workers and pass on. As we wonder about we find many churches and chapels; and perhaps we come after a while to a great "cathedral" or bishop's church, rearing its lofty roof to the sky. No pains have been spared to make this as grand and imposing as possible; and we gaze upon its great height with awe, and wonder at the marvelously quaint and clever patterns in which the stone is carved.

We leave this also after a time; and then we come to the "belfrey" or townhall. This is the real center of the life of the city. Here is the strong square tower, like the "donjon" of a castle, where the townsmen may make their last stand in case an enemy succeeds in entering their walls, and they cannot beat him back in their narrow streets.

On top of the tower is the bell, with watchmen always on the lookout to give the signal in case of fire or danger. The bell is also used for more peaceful purposes, as it gives the signal each morning and evening for the workmen all over the city to begin and to quit work; and it also summons the citizens from time to time, to public meetings. Also every night at eight or nine o'clock, it sounds the "curfew" (French *couvre feu*, "cover fire") as a signal to cover the fire with ashes and cease the day's labors.

Within the tower are dungeons for prisoners, and meeting rooms for the rulers of the city. There also are strong rooms where the city money is kept, together with the city seal. Lastly there is the charter which gives the city its liberties; this is the most precious of all the city possessions.

Even in ordinary times the city presents a bustling, busy appearance. If it is a city which holds a fair once or twice a year, what shall we say of it then? For several weeks at such times the city is one vast store. Strange merchants come from all parts of the land and set up their booths and stalls along the streets, and the city shops are crowded with goods. For miles about the people throng in to buy the things they need.

Above is a picture of the streets of a city during fair-time in the thirteenth century. In the middle of the picture we see a townsman and his wife returning home after making their purchases. Behind them are a knight and his attendant, on horseback, picking their way through the crowd. On the right hand side of the street is the shop of a cloth merchant; and we see the merchant and his wife showing goods to customers, while workmen are unpacking a box in the street. Next door is a tavern, with its sign hung out; and near this we see a cross which some pious person has erected at the street corner. On the left-hand side of the street we see a cripple begging for alms. Back of him is another cloth-merchant's shop; and next to this is a money-changer's table, where a group of people are having money weighed to see that there is no cheating in the payment. Beyond this is an elevated stage, on which a company of tumblers and jugglers are performing, with a crowd of people about them. In the background we see some tall-roofed houses, topped with turrets, and beyond these we can just make out the spire of a church rising to the sky.

This is indeed a busy scene; and it is a picture which we may carry away with us. It well shows the energy and the activity which, during the later Middle Ages, made the towns the starting place for so many important movements.

Life of the Monastery

In the last three chapters we have studied the life of the castle, of the village, and of the town. We must now see what the life of the monastery was like.

In the Middle Ages men thought that storms and lightning, famine and sickness, were signs of the wrath of God, or were the work of evil spirits. The world was a terrible place to them, and the wickedness and misery with which it was filled made them long to escape from it. Also, they felt that God was pleased when they voluntarily led lives of hardship and self-denial, for his sake. So great numbers of men went out into the desert places and became hermits or monks, in order that they might better serve God and save their own souls.

Soon the separate monks drew together and formed monasteries, or groups of monks living in communities, according to certain rules. A famous monk named Benedict drew up a series of rules for his monastery, and these served the purpose so well that they were adopted for many others. In course of time the monasteries of all Western Europe were put under "the Benedictine rule," as it was called.

The dress of the monks was to be of coarse woolen cloth, with a cowl or hood which could be pulled up to protect the head; and about the waist a cord was worn for a girdle. The gown of the Benedictines was usually black, so they were called "black monks." As the centuries went by, new orders were founded, with new rules; but these usually took the rule of St. Benedict and merely changed it to meet new conditions. In this way arose "white monks," and monks of other names.

In addition, orders of "friars" were founded, especially by St. Francis and St. Dominic. These were like the monks in many ways, but lived more in the world, preaching, teaching, and caring for the sick. These were called "black friars," "gray friars," or "white friars," according to the color of their dress.

Besides the orders for men, there were also orders of "nuns" for women. St. Scholastica, the friend of St. Benedict, and St. Clara, the friend of St. Francis, were the founders of two important orders of nuns. In some places in the Middle Ages nunneries became almost as common as monasteries.

Let us try now to see what a Benedictine monastery was like. One of the Benedict's rules provided that every monastery should be so arranged that everything the monks needed would be in the monastery itself, and there would be no need to wander about outside; "for this," said Benedict, "is not at all good for their souls." Each monastery, therefore, became a settlement complete in itself. It not only had its halls where the monks ate and slept, and its own church; it also had its own mill, its own bake-oven, and its own workshops where the monks made the things they needed.

The better to shut out the world, and to protect the monastery against robbers, the buildings were surrounded by a strong wall. Outside this lay the fields of the monastery, where the monks themselves raised the grain they needed, or which were tilled for them by peasants in the same way that the lands of the lords were tilled. Finally, there was the woodland, where the swine were herded; and the pasture lands, where the cattle and sheep were sent to graze.

The amount of land belonging to a monastery was often quite large. Nobles and kings frequently gave gifts of land, and the monks in return prayed for their souls. Often when the land came into the possession of the monks, it was covered with swamps or forests; but by unwearying labor the swamps were drained and the forests felled; and soon smiling fields appeared where before there was only a wilderness.

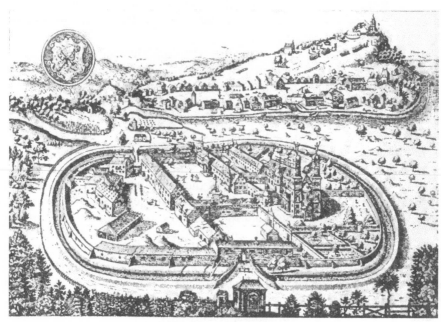

A German monastery

Above is the picture of a German monastery, at the close of the Middle Ages. There we see the strong wall, surrounded by a ditch, inclosing the buildings, and protecting the monastery from attack. To enter the enclosure we must cross the bridge and present ourselves at the gate. When we have passed this we see to the left stables for cattle and horses, while to the right are gardens of herbs for the cure of the sick. Near by is the monks' graveyard with the graves marked by little crosses.

In the center of the enclosure are workshops, where the monks work at different trades. The tall building with the spires crowned with the figures of saints, is the church, where the monks hold services at regular intervals throughout the day and night.

Adjoining this, in the form of a square, are the buildings in which the monks sleep and eat. This is the "cloister," and is the principal part of the monastery. In southern lands this inner square or cloister was usually surrounded on all sides by a porch or piazza, the roof of which was supported on long rows of pillars; and here the monks might pace to and fro in quiet talk when the duties of worship and labor did not occupy their time.

In addition to these buildings, there are many others which we cannot stop to describe. Some are used to carry on the work of the monastery; some are for the use of the abbot, who is the ruler of the monks; some are hospitals for the sick; and some are guest chambers, where travellers are lodged over night.

In the guest chambers the travellers might sleep undisturbed all the night through. It was not so with the monks. They must begin their worship long before the sun was up. Soon after midnight the bell of the monastery rings, the monks rise from their hard beds, and gather in the church, to recite prayers, read portions of the Bible, and sing psalms. Not less than twelve of the psalms of the Old Testament must be read each night

A French cloister

at this service. At daybreak again the bell rings, and once more the monks gather in the church. This is the first of the seven services which are held during the day. The others come at seven o'clock in the morning, at nine o'clock, at noon, at three in the afternoon, at six o'clock, and at bed-time. At each of these there are prayers, reading from the Scriptures, and chanting of psalms. Latin was the only language used in the church services of the West in the Middle Ages; so the Bible was read, the psalms sung, and the prayers recited in this tongue. The services are so arranged that in the course of every week the entire Psalter or psalm book is gone through; then, at the Sunday night service, they begin again.

Besides these services, there are many other things which the monks must do. "Idleness," wrote St. Benedict, "is the enemy of the soul." So it was arranged that at fixed hours during the day the monks should labor with their hands. Some plowed the fields, harrowed them, and planted and harvested the grain. Others worked at various trades in the workshops of the monasteries. If any brother

Monk in scriptorium

showed too much pride in his work, and put himself above the others because of his skill, he was made to work at something else. The monks must be humble at all times. "A monk," said Benedict, "must always show humility,—not only in his heart, but with his body also. This is so whether he is at work, or at prayer; whether he is in the monastery, in the garden, in the road, or in the fields. Everywhere,—sitting, walking, or standing,—let him always be with head bowed, his looks fixed upon the ground; and let him remember every hour that he is guilty of his sins."

One of the most useful labors which the monks performed was the copying and writing of books. At certain hours of the day, especially on Sundays, the brothers were required by Benedict's rule to read and to study. In the Middle Ages, of course, there were no printing presses, and all books were "manuscript," that is, they were copied a letter at a time by hand. So in each well-regulated monastery there was a writing-room, or "scriptorium," where some of the monks worked copying manuscripts.

The writing was usually done on skins of parchment. These the monks cut to the size of the page, rubbing the surface smooth with pumice stone. Then the margins were marked and the lines ruled with sharp awls. The writing was done with pens made of quills or of reeds, and with ink made of soot mixed with gum and acid.

The greatest care was used in forming each letter, and at the beginning of the chapters a large initial was made. Sometimes these initials were really pictures, beautifully "illuminated" in blue, gold, and crimson. All this required skill and much pains.

"He who does not know how to write," wrote one monk at the end of a manuscript, "imagines that it is no labor; but though only three fingers hold the pen, the whole body grows weary." And another one wrote: "I pray you, good readers who may use this book, do not forget him who copied it. It was a poor brother named Louis, who while he copied the volume (which was brought from a foreign country) endured the cold, and was obliged to finish in the night what he could not write by day."

The monks, by copying books, did a great service to the world, for it was in this way that many valuable works were preserved during the Dark Ages, when violence and ignorance spread, and the love of learning had almost died out.

In other ways, also, the monks helped the cause of learning. At a time when no one else took the trouble, or knew how, to write a history of the things that were going on, the monks in most of the great monasteries wrote "annals" or "chronicles" in which events were each year set down. And at a time when there were no schools except those provided by the Church, the monks taught boys to read and to write, so that there might always be learned men to carry on the work of religion. The education which they gave, and the books which they wrote, were, of course, in Latin, like the services of the Church; for this was the only language of educated men.

The histories which the monks wrote were, no doubt, very poor ones, and the schools were not very good; but they were ever so much better than none at all. Here is what a monk wrote in the "annals" of his monastery, as the history of the year 807; it will show us something about both the histories and the schools:

"807. Grimoald, duke of Beneventum, died; and there was great sickness in the monastery of St. Boniface, so that many of the younger brothers died. The boys of the monastery school beat their teacher and ran away."

That is all we are told. Were the boys just unruly and naughty? Did they rebel at the tasks of school at a time when Charlemagne was waging his mighty wars; and did they long to become knights and warriors instead of priests and monks? Or was it on account of the sickness that they ran away? We cannot tell. That is the way it is with many things in the Middle Ages. Most of what we know about the history of that time we learn from the "chronicles" kept by the monks, and these do not tell us nearly all that we should like to know.

The three most important things which were required of the monks were that they should have no property of their own, that they should not marry, and that they should obey those who were placed over them. "A monk," said Benedict, "should have absolutely nothing, neither a book, nor a tablet, nor a pen." Even the clothes which they wore were the property of the monastery. If any gifts were sent them by their friends or relatives, they must turn them over to the abbot for the use of the monastery as a whole.

The rule of obedience required that a monk, when ordered to do a thing, should do it without delay; and if impossible things were commanded, he must at least make the attempt.

The rule about marrying was equally strict; and in some monasteries it was counted a sin even to look upon a woman.

Other rules forbade the monks to talk at certain times of the day and in their sleeping halls. For fear they might forget themselves at the table, St. Benedict ordered that one of the brethren should always read aloud at meals from some holy book. All were required to live on the simplest and plainest food. The rules, indeed, were so strict, that it was often difficult to enforce them, especially after the monasteries became rich and powerful. Then, although the monks might not have any property of their own, they enjoyed vast riches belonging to the monastery as a whole, and often lived in luxury and idleness. When this happened there was usually a reaction, and new orders arose with stricter and stricter rules. So we have times of zeal and strict enforcement of the rules, followed by periods of decay; and these, in turn, followed by new periods of strictness. This went on to the close of the Middle Ages, when most of the monasteries were done away with.

When any one wished to become a monk, he had first to go through a trial. He must become a "novice" and live in a monastery, under its rules, for a year; then if he was still of the same mind, he took the vows of Poverty, Chastity, and Obedience. "From that day forth," says the rule of St. Benedict, "he shall not be allowed to depart from the monastery, nor to shake from his neck the yoke of the Rule; for, after so long delay, he was at liberty either to receive it or to refuse it."

When the monasteries had become corrupt, some men no doubt became monks in order that they might live in idleness and luxury. But let us think rather of the many men who became monks because they believed that this was the best way to serve God.

Let us think, in closing, of one of the best of the monasteries of the Middle Ages, and let us look at its life through the eyes of a noble young novice. The monastery was in France, and its abbot, St. Bernard, was famous throughout the Christian world, in the twelfth century, for his piety and zeal. Of this monastery the novice writes.

"I watch the monks at their daily services, and at their nightly vigils from midnight to the dawn; and as I hear them singing so holily and unwearyingly, they seem to me more like angels than men. Some of them have been bishops or rulers, or else have been famous for their rank and knowledge; now all are equal, and no one is higher or lower than any other. I see them in the gardens with the hoe, in the meadows with fork and rake, in the forests with the ax. When I remember what they have been, and consider their present condition and work, their poor and ill-made clothes, my heart tells me that they are not the dull and speechless beings they seem, but that their life is hid with Christ in the heavens.

"Farewell! God willing, on the next Sunday after Ascension Day, I too, shall put on the armor of my profession as a monk!"

Triumph of Papacy over Empire

We have seen, in another chapter, how the bishop of Rome became the head of the Western Church, with the title of Pope; and we have seen how Charlemagne restored the position of Emperor as ruler of the West. We must now follow the history of these two great institutions,—the Papacy and the Empire,—and see how they got along together.

After Gregory the Great died, it was long before the Church had a Pope who was so able and good; and after Charlemagne was dead, it was long before there was another Emperor as great as he had been. Charlemagne's empire was divided by his grandsons, as we have seen, into three kingdoms; and though the oldest of them received the title of Emperor, he had little of Charlemagne's power. Afterwards the descendants of Charlemagne grew weaker and weaker, and finally their power came entirely to an end. We have already seen how their rule ceased in France and the power passed to the family of that Count Odo who defended Paris so bravely against the Northmen in the year 886. In Italy and Germany also, at about the same time, the rule of the "Carolingians" ceased, and new rulers arose.

In Germany it was the Saxons, whom Charlemagne had conquered with so much difficulty, who now took the leading part in the government. A new and stronger German kingdom was established, and then of these Saxon kings— Otto I., who was rightly called Otto the Great—gained the rule over Italy also.

When this was done, he revived the title of Emperor, which meant something more than King. It meant not only the rule over Italy and Germany, but also a supremacy over all the kings of Western Europe, such as Charlemagne had exercised. This occurred in the year 962. Otto had already been King for twenty-six years, and he ruled for twelve years longer, proving to be as great a ruler as Emperor as he had been as King.

One of the first things he did in Italy was to put the Papacy in a better condition. During the troubled times that had followed the fall of Charlemagne's empire, Italian nobles oppressed teh popes and even attempted to set them up and pull them down at pleasure. The Papacy had no army of its own, and when there was no one who was acknowledged as Emperor there was no one to whom the Pope could turn for aid. When Otto I. revived the Empire, it became his duty to protect the Pope. After many efforts the emperors succeeded in taking from the Italian nobles their power, and soon the position of Pope was higher than it had ever been.

Then the question arose as to what their relation should be towards the emperors.

Just one hundred years after the death of Otto I., a man became Pope who had very decided opinions on this subject. His name was Hildebrand. He was the son of a poor carpenter, and was born in Italy, but he was of German origin. His uncle was the head of a monastery of Rome, and it was there that the boy was brought up and educated. When he became a man, he too became a monk. Circumstances soon led him to France, and there for a while he was a member of the most famous monastery of Europe—the one at Cluny, in Burgundy.

Not only the Papacy, but the whole Church, had fallen into a bad condition at this time. Monks had ceased to obey the rules made for their government, and lived idly and often wickedly. Priests and bishops, instead of giving their attention to the churches which were under their care, spent their time like the nobles of that day, in hunting, in pleasure, and in war.

There were three evils which were especially complained of.

First, priests, bishops, and even popes, often got their offices by purchase instead of being freely elected or appointed; this was called "simony."

Second, the greater part of the clergy had followed the example of the Eastern Church, and married, so breaking the rule of "celibacy," which required that they should not marry. This was especially harmful, because the married clergy sought to provide for their children by giving them lands and other property belonging to the Church.

The third evil was the "investiture" of clergymen by laymen. When a bishop, for example, was chosen, he was given the staff and the ring, which were the signs of his office, by the emperor or king, instead of by an archbishop; and this "investiture" by laymen made the clergy look more to the rulers of the land than to the rulers of the Church.

The monastery of Cluny took the leading part in fighting against these evils. Its abbots joined to it other monasteries, which were purified and re-formed, and in this way Cluny became the head of a "congregation" or union of monasteries which numbered many hundreds. Everywhere it raised the cry, "No simony;—celibacy;—and no lay investiture!"

When Hildebrand came to Cluny this movement had been going on for some time, and much good had already been done. But it was through the efforts of Hildebrand himself that the movement was to win its greatest success.

After staying at Cluny for some months, Hildebrand returned to Rome. There for almost a quarter of a century, under five successive popes, he was the chief adviser and helper of the Papacy. Several times the people of Rome wished to make Hildebrand Pope, but he refused. At last, when the fifth of these popes had died, he was forced to submit. In the midst of the funeral services, a cry arose from the clergy and the people:

"Hildebrand is Pope! St. Peter chooses Hildebrand to be Pope!"

When Hildebrand sought again to refuse the office, his voice was drowned in cries:

"It is the will of St. Peter! Hildebrand is Pope!"

So he was obliged at last to submit. Unwillingly, it is said, and with tears in his eyes, he was led to the papal throne. There he was clothed with the scarlet robe, and crowned with the papal crown; then, at length, he was seated in the chair of St. Peter, where so many popes had sat before him. In accordance with the custom, he now took a new name, and as Pope he was always called Gregory VII.

The Emperor at this time was Henry IV., who had been ruler over Germany ever since he was six years old. One of his guardians had let the boy have his own way in everything; so, although he was well meaning, he had grown up without self control, and with many bad habits. Gregory was determined to make the Emperor give up the right of investiture, and also tried to force him to reform his manner of living. Henry, for his part, was just as determined never to give up any right which the emperors had had before him, and complained bitterly of the pride and haughtiness of the Pope.

A quarrel was the result, which lasted for almost fifty years. The question to be settled was not merely the right of investiture. It included also the question whether the Emperor was above the Pope, or the Pope above the Emperor. Charlemagne and Otto I., and other emperors, had often come into Italy to correct popes when they did wrong; and at times they had even set aside evil popes, and named new ones in their place. Gregory now claimed that the Pope was above the Emperor; that the lay power had no rights over the clergy; and that the Pope might even depose an Emperor and free his subjects from the obedience which they owed him. The Pope, he said, had given the Empire to Charlemagne, and what one Pope had given another could take away.

The popes relied, in such struggles, on the power which they possessed to "excommunicate" a person. Excommunication cut the person off from the Church, and no good Christian, thenceforth, might have anything to do with him. They could not live with him, nor do business with him; and if he died unforgiving, his soul was believed to be lost. This was the weapon which Gregory used against the Emperor Henry, when he refused to give up the right of investiture. He excommunicated him, and forbade all people from obeying him as Emperor, or having anything to do with him. Henry's subjects were already dissatisfied with his rule, so they took this occasion to rise in rebellion.

Soon Henry saw that unless he made his peace with the Pope he would lose his whole kingdom. So with his wife and infant son, and only one attendant, he crossed the Alps in the depth of winter. After terrible hardships, he arrived at Canossa, where the Pope was staying, on January 25, 1076. There, for three days, with bare feet and in the dress of a penitent, he was forced to stand in the snow before the gate of the castle. On the fourth day he was admitted to the presence of the Pope; and crying, "Holy Father, spare me!" he threw himself at Gregory's feet. Then the Pope raised him up and forgave him; and after promising that henceforth he would rule in all things as the Pope wished, Henry was allowed to return to Germany.

Henry IV at Canossa

This, however did not end the quarrel. Henry could not forgive the humiliation that had been put upon him. The German people and clergy, too, would not admit the rights which the Pope claimed. Gradually Henry recovered the power which he had lost; and at last he again went to Italy,—this time with an army at his back. All Gregory's enemies now rose up against him, and the Pope was obliged to flee to the Normans in Southern Italy. There the gray-haired old Pope soon died, saying:

"One thing only fills me with hope. I have always loved the law of God, and hated evil. Therefore I die in exile."

Even after the death of Gregory the struggle went on. New popes arose who claimed all the power that Gregory had claimed; and everywhere the monks of Cluny aided the Pope, and opposed the Emperor. Henry's son, too, rebelled against him, and at last, twenty years after the death of Gregory, Henry IV. died broken-hearted and deprived of power.

When once Henry's son had become Emperor, he found that he must continue the struggle, or his power would be nothing. At last it was seen that each side must give up something, so a compromise was agreed to. The Emperor, it was settled, should surrender his claim to give the bishops the ring and the staff. On the other hand, the Pope agreed that the Emperor might control the election of bishops, and bind them to perform the duties which they owed as a result of the lands which they received from him. The whole trouble had arisen from the fact that the bishops were not only officers of the Church, but that they held feudal "benefices" of the Emperor. By a compromise which was agreed to in the year 1122, the Emperor surrendered his claim to give the bishops the ring and the staff. On the other hand, the Pope agreed that the Emperor might control the election of bishops, and bind them to perform the duties which they owed as a result of the lands which they received from him.

This, however, did not settle the question whether the Pope was above the Emperor or the Emperor above the Pope. On this point there continued to be trouble throughout the Middle Ages.

Decline of the Papal Power

Everybody in the Middle Ages agreed that there must be one head to rule over the Church, and one head, above all kings and princes, to rule over the states of Europe; but they could not settle the relations which these two should bear to each other.

Some said that the power of the Pope in the world was like the soul of a man, and power of the Emperor was like his body; and since the soul was greater than the body, so the Pope must be above the Emperor.

Another argument was founded on the passage in the Bible in which the apostles said to Christ: "Behold, here are two swords;" and Christ answered, "It is enough." By the two swords, it was claimed, was meant the power of the Pope, and the power of the Emperor. Those in favor of the Papacy tried to explain that both the swords were in Peter's hands, and that as Peter was the founder of the Papacy, Christ meant both powers to be under the Pope.

Still another argument was based on the "two great lights" (the sun and the moon) which the Bible tells us God set, the one to rule the day, and the other the night. The sun, it was said, represented the Pope, and the moon the Emperor, and since the moon shines only by light received from the sun, so, it was argued, the Emperor's power must be drawn entirely from the Pope. It is not surprising that those who favored the Emperor would not accept arguments like these.

When Frederick Barbarossa was Emperor there was another long quarrel; and one of the Pope's officers tried to show that Frederick held the Empire as a "benefice" from the Pope, just as a vassal held his land as a benefice from his lord. This claim raised such an outburst of anger from the Germans, that the Pope was obliged to explain it away.

The last great struggle between the Papacy and Empire came when Frederick II., the grandson of Frederick Barbarossa, was Emperor. Frederick II. ruled not only over Germany and Northern Italy, but over Southern Italy as well. His mother was the heiress of the last of the Norman kings in Italy; and from her Frederick inherited the kingdom of the Two Sicilies. The pope was afraid that the Emperor might try to get Rome also, so a quarrel soon broke out.

Frederick had taken the cross and promised to go on a crusade. When he delayed doing this, the Pope

Seizure of Pope Boniface VIII

excommunicated him for not going. Frederick at last was ready, and went to the Holy Land. Then the Pope excommunicated him a second time for going without getting the excommunication removed. In the Holy Land Frederick had great trouble with the Pope's friends because he was excommunicated. At last he made a treaty by which he recovered Jerusalem from the Mohammedans, and returned home Then he was excommunicated a third time. It seemed as if there was nothing that he could do that would please the Pope.

For a while peace was made between the Pope and Emperor; but it did not last long. The Papacy could never be content so long as the Emperor ruled over Southern Italy. A new quarrel broke out; and this time it lasted until Frederick's death in the year 1250. After that, the struggle continued until the Papacy was completely victorious, and Frederick's sons and grandson were slain, and Southern Italy was ruled by a king who was not, also, the ruler of Germany.

Thus the Papacy was left completely victorious over the Empire. For nearly a quarter of a century there was then no real Emperor in Germany; and when at last one was chosen he was careful to leave Italy alone. "Italy," said he, "is the den of the lion. I see many tracks leading into it, but there are none coming out." From this time on the Emperor of the Holy Roman Empire comes more and more to be merely the ruler over Germany.

At about the same time the Popes began to make greater claims than ever. One Pope, Boniface VIII., clothed himself in the imperial cloak, and with the scepter in his hand and a crown upon his head, cried: "I am Pope; I am Emperor!" This could not last long. The Empire was gone, but there were now new national governments arising in France, England, and elsewhere, which were conscious of their strength.

If we go back to the beginning of the Middle Ages, we find that the peoples who were overthrowing the old Roman Empire were bound together in *tribes*, the members of which were united by ties of kinship, that is, they were all of the same blood. But as time went on, and the different peoples settled down to orderly life, the old tribes were broken up. Then men entered into feudal relationships by becoming the vassals of their lords, and thenceforth the ties which bound them together were those of loyalty and feudal service. As yet there was no feeling of patriotism among them, or of loyalty to a country. After the Crusades the kings gained more power, and began to take from the nobles their feudal rights of raising armies, making war when they pleased, holding courts, and the like. In this way strong national government arose in France, in England, and elsewhere; and it was not long before these also came into conflict with the Papacy.

The most powerful of these new governments was the monarchy of France. Pope Boniface VIII., who had made such great claims for the Papacy, soon got into a quarrel with Philip IV., of that country, about some money matters; and the way he was treated by the servants of the King showed that the old power of the popes was gone, equally with the power of the emperors. Boniface was seized at the little town in Italy where he was staying, was struck in the face with the glove of one of his own nobles, and was kept prisoner for several days. Although he was soon released, the old Pope died in a few weeks,—of shame and anger, it was said.

Nor was this the end of the matter. Within a few months the seat of the Papacy was changed from Rome to Avignon, on the river Rhone. There, for nearly seventy years, the popes remained under the influence of the kings of France. This period is known as the "Babylonian captivity" of the Papacy, in memory of the seventy years' captivity of the Jews at Babylon, which is described in the Old Testament.

And even when, at last, a Pope removed the Papacy back to Rome, new troubles arose. A great division or "schism" followed, during which there were two popes instead of one; and all the nations of Europe were divided as to whether they should obey the Pope at Rome, or the one at Avignon.

"All our West land," wrote an Englishman named Wiclif, "is with that one Pope or that other; and he that is with that one, hateth the other, with all his. Some men say that here is the Pope at Avignon, for he was well chosen; and some men say that he is yonder at Rome, for he was first chosen."

A council of the Church tried to end the schism; but it only made matters worse by adding a third Pope to the two that already existed. At last, another and greater council was held; and there, after the schism had lasted for nearly forty years, all three popes were set aside, and a new one chosen whom all the nations accepted.

So, at last, the Papacy was re-united and restored to Rome. But it never recovered entirely from its stay at Avignon, and from the Great Schism. The power of the popes was never again as great as it had been before the quarrel between Boniface VIII. and the King of France. The Papacy had triumphed over the Empire, but it could not triumph over the national kingdoms.

"We look on Pope and Emperor alike," said a writer in the fifteenth century, who soon became Pope himself, "as names in a story, or heads in a picture."

Thenceforth there was no ruler whom all Christendom would obey. The end of the Middle Ages, indeed, was fast approaching. The modern times, when each nation obeys its own kings, and follows only its own interests, were close at hand.

First Period of the Hundred Years' War

One of the signs that the Middle Ages were coming to an end was the long war between France and England. It lasted altogether from 1337 to 1453, and is called the Hundred Years' War.

When William the Conqueror became King of England, he did not cease to be Duke of Normandy. Indeed, as time went on, the power of the English kings in France increased, until William's successors ruled all the western part of that land, from north of the river Seine to the Pyrenees Mountains, and from the Bay of Biscay almost to the river Rhone. They held all this territory as fiefs of the kings of France; but the fact that they were also independent kings of England made them stronger than their overlords. This led to frequent wars, until, at last, the English kings had lost all their land in France except Aquitaine, in the southwest.

These, however, were merely feudal wars between the rulers of the two countries. They did not much concern the people of either France or England; for in neither country had the people come to feel that they were a nation and that one of their first duties was to love their own country and support their own government. In Aquitaine, indeed, the people scarcely felt that they were French at all, and rather preferred the kings of England to the French kings who dwelt at Paris.

During the Hundred Years' War, all this was to change. In fighting with one another, in this long struggle, the people of France and of England came gradually to feel that they *were* French and English. The people of Aquitaine began to feel that they were of nearer kin to those who dwelt about Paris than they were to the English, and began to feel love for France and hatred for England. It was the same, too, with the English. In fighting the French, the descendants of the old Saxons, and of the conquering Normans, came to feel that they were all alike Englishmen. So, although the long war brought terrible suffering and misery, it brought also some good to both countries. In each patriotism was born, and in each the people became a nation.

There were many things which led up to the war, but the chief was the fact that the French King, who died in 1328, left no son to succeed him. The principal claimants for the throne were his cousin, Philip, who was Duke of Valois, and his nephew, Edward III. of England. The French nobles decided in favor of Duke Philip, and he became King as Philip VI. Edward did not like this decision, but he accepted it for a time. After nine years, however, war broke out because of other reasons; and then Edward claimed the throne as his of right.

During the first eight years, neither country gained any great advantage, though the English won an important battle at sea. In the ninth year the English gained their first great victory on land.

Archers shooting at mark

This battle took place at Crecy, in the northernmost part of France, about one hundred miles from Paris. The French army was twice as large as the English, and was made up mainly of mounted knights, armed with lance and sword, and clad in the heavy armor of the Middle Ages. The English army was made up chiefly of archers on foot. Everywhere in England boys were trained from the time they were six or seven years old at shooting with the bow and arrow. As they grew older, stronger and stronger bows were given them, until at last they could use the great longbows of their fathers. The greatest care was taken in this teaching; and on holidays grown men as well as boys might be seen practicing shooting at marks on the village commons. In this way the English became the best archers in Europe, and so powerful were their bows that the arrows would often pierce armor or slay a knight's horse at a hundred yards.

So the advantage was not so great on the side of the French as it seemed. Besides, King Edward placed his men very skillfully, while the French managed the battle very badly. Edward placed his archers at the top of a sloping hillside, with the knights behind. In command of the first line he placed his fifteen-year-old son, the Black Prince, while the King himself took a position on a little windmill-hill in the rear.

The French had a large number of crossbowmen with them. Although the crossbowmen could not shoot so rapidly as the English archers, because the crossbow had to be rested on the ground, and wound up after each shot, they could shoot to a greater distance and with more force. Unluckily, a shower wet the strings of the crossbows, while the English were able to protect their bows and keep the strings dry. So when the French King ordered the crossbowmen to advance, they went unwillingly; and when the English archers, each

A crossbowman

stepping forward one pace, let fly their arrows, the crossbowmen turned and fled.

At this King Philip was very angry, for he thought they fled through cowardice; so he cried:

"Slay me those rascals!"

At this command, the French knights rode among the crossbowmen and killed many of their own men. All this while the English arrows were falling in showers about them, and many horses, and knights, as well as archers, were slain.

Then the French horsemen charged the English lines. Some of the knights about the young Prince now began to fear for him, and sent to the King, urging him to send assistance.

"Is my son dead," asked the King, "or so wounded that he cannot help himself?"

"No, sire, please God," answered the messenger, "but he is in a hard passage of arms, and much needs your help."

"Then," said King Edward, "return to them that sent you, and tell them not to send to me again so long as my son lives. I command them to let the boy win his spurs. If God be pleased, I will that the honor of this day shall be his."

On the French side was the blind old King of Bohemia. When the fighting began he said to those about him:

"You are my vassals and friends. I pray you to lead me so far into the battle that I may strike at least one good stroke with my sword!"

Knights in battle

Two of his attendants then placed themselves on either side of him; and, tying the bridles of their horses together, they rode into the fight. There the old blind King fought valiantly; and when the battle was over, the bodies of all three were found, with their horses still tied together.

The victory of the English was complete. Thousands of the French were slain, and King Philip himself was obliged to flee to escape capture. But though the Black Prince won his spurs right nobly, the chief credit for the victory was due to the English archers.

It was some years after this before the next great battle was fought. This was due, in part, to a terrible sickness which came upon all Western Europe soon after the battle of Crecy. It was called the Black Death, and arose in Asia, where cholera and the plague often arise. Whole villages were attacked at the same time; and for two years the disease raged everywhere. When, at last, it died out, half of the population of England was gone; and France had suffered almost as terribly.

Ten years after the battle of Crecy (in 1356) the war broke out anew. The Black Prince, at the head of an army, set out from Aquitaine and marched northward into the heart of France. Soon, however, he found his retreat cut off near the city of Poitiers by the French King John (who had succeeded his father Philip), with an army six or seven times the size of the English force. The situation of the English was so bad that the Prince offered to give up all the prisoners, castles, and towns which they had taken during this expedition, and to promise not to fight against France again for seven years, if the French King would grant them a free retreat. But King John felt so sure of victory that he refused these terms. Then the battle began.

Just as at Crecy, the English were placed on a little hill; and again they depended chiefly on their archers. From behind a thick hedge they shot their arrows in clouds as the French advanced. Soon all was uproar and confusion. Many of the French lay wounded or slain; and many of their horses, feeling the sting of the arrow-heads, reared wildly, flung their riders, and dashed to the rear. When once dismounted, a knight could not mount to the saddle again without assistance, so heavy was the armor which was then worn.

In a short time this division of the French was overthrown. Then a second, and finally a third division met the same fate. To the war-cries, "Mountjoy! Saint Denis!" the English replied with shouts of "St. George! Guyenne!" The ringing of spear-heads upon shields, the noise of breaking lances, the clash of hostile swords and battle-axes, were soon added to the rattle of English arrows upon French breastplates and helmets. At last the French were all overthrown, or turned in flight, except in one quarter of the field. There King John, with a few of his bravest knights, fought valiantly on foot. As he swung his heavy battle-ax, now at this foe and now at that, his son Philip,—a brave boy of thirteen years,—cried unceasingly:

"Father, guard right! Father, guard left!"

Finally even the King was obliged to surrender; and he and his son Philip were taken prisoners to the tent of the English Prince. There they were courteously entertained, the Prince waiting upon them at table with his own hands. But for several years they remained captives, awaiting the ransom which the English demanded.

Middle Period of the Struggle

The battle of Poitiers was a sad blow indeed to France. Many hundreds of her noblest knights were there slain; and all sorts of disorders arose during the captivity of her King. The peasants rose in rebellion against their masters, and civil war broke out. And when, after four years of comfortable captivity, King John was set free, he was obliged to pay a heavy ransom and sign a peace in which he surrendered to the English, in full right, all of Aquitaine.

Soon after this "Good King John," as he was called, died, leaving his kingdom in great disorder He was a good knight and brave man; but he was a poor general and a weak king.

His eldest son, Charles, who was styled Charles V., or Charles the Wise, now became King. He was very different from his father; and though he was not nearly so knightly a warrior, he proved a much better king. He improved the government and the army; and when the war with the English began again, he at once began to be successful.

The Black Prince was now broken in health, and died in the year 1376; the old English King, Edward III., died the next year; and then Richard II., the twelve-year-old son of the Black Prince, became King of England. Troubles, too, broke out in England, so the English were not able to carry on the war as vigorously as they had done before.

Knight attacking foot-soldiers

At the same time the French King found a general named Du Guesclin, who proved to be one of the best commanders that the Middle Ages produced.

Du Guesclin was a poor country noble, from Western France. As a boy he was so ugly and ill favored that his parents scarcely loved him, and his chief pleasure was in fighting the village lads. At sixteen years of age he ran away from home, and lived for a time with an uncle. He longed to take part in tournaments and perform feats of arms, but he was too poor to provide himself with a horse and armor. But one day, when a tournament was being held at his native town, he returned there, borrowed a horse and armor, and overthrew fifteen knights, one after the other. When he raised the visor of his helmet, and his father saw who the unknown warrior was, there was a happy reunion.

In the earlier stages of the Hundred Years' War, Du Guesclin had taken some part, but had not been present at either Crecy or at Poitiers. He had made a name form himself, however, and was recognized as a man of importance.

When Charles V. renewed the war with the English, he chose Du Guesclin to be "Constable of France," that is, commander-in-chief of the French armies. At first Du Guesclin asked the King to excuse him from this office, saying that he was but a poor man, and not of high birth; and how could he expect the great nobles of France to obey him? But the King answered him, saying:

"Sir, do not excuse yourself thus; for there is no nobleman in the kingdom, even among my own kin, who would not obey you. And if any should be so hardy as to do otherwise, he would surely hear from me. So take the office freely, I beseech you."

So Du Guesclin became Constable, and from that time the fortunes of France began to improve.

One trouble with the French had been that they scorned the "base-born" foot-soldiers, and thought that war should be the business of the heavy-armed knights alone; and another was that the knights thought it disgraceful to retreat, even when they knew they could not win. With Du Geusclin, all this was different. He was willing to use peasants and townsmen if their way of fighting was better than that of the nobles; and he did not think it beneath him to retreat, when he saw that he could not win a victory.

So, by caution and good sense, and the support of wise King Charles, he won victory after victory; and though no great battles were fought, almost all of the English possessions in France came once more into the hands of the French.

But here, for a time, the French successes stopped. Du Guesclin died, in 1380, and soon after him King Charles V. Now it was the French who had a boy king, and when this King, Charles VI., grew to be a man, he became insane. His uncles quarreled with one another and with the King's brother for the government. Soon the quarrel led to murder, and the murder to civil war; and again France was thrown into all the misery and disorder from which it had been rescued by Charles the Wise.

In England, about this time, King Henry V., came to the throne. He was a young and warlike prince; and he wished, through a renewal of the war, to win glory for himself. Besides, he remembered the old claim of Edward III., to the French crown; and he thought that now, when the French nobles were fighting among

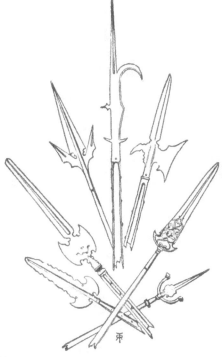

Halberds, bills, and pikes

themselves, was a fine opportunity to make that claim good.

So, in the year 1415, King Henry landed with an army in France, and began again the old, old struggle. And again, after a few months, the English found their retreat cut off near a little village called Agincourt, by a much larger army of the French. But King Henry remembered the victories of Crecy and Poitiers, and did not despair. When one of his knights wished that the thousands of warriors then lying idle in England were only there, King Henry exclaimed:

"I would not have a single man more. If God gives us the victory, it will be plain that we owe it to His grace. If not, the fewer we are, the less loss to England."

At Agincourt there was no sheltering hedge to protect the English archers. To make up for this, King Henry ordered each man to provide himself with tall stakes, sharpened at each end; these they planted slantwise in the ground as a protection against French horsemen. Most of the English force was again made up of archers with the long-bow, while most of the French were knights in full armor. The French, indeed, seemed to have forgotten all that Du Guesclin and Charles V., had taught them. To make matters worse, their knights dismounted and sought to march upon the English position on foot. As the field through which they had to pass was newly plowed and wet with rain, the heavy-armed knights sank knee deep in mud at every step.

For the third time the English victory was complete. Eleven thousand Frenchmen were left dead upon the field, and among the number were more than a hundred great lords and princes.

In after years Englishmen sang of the wonderful victory in these words:

> "Agincourt, Agincourt!
> Know ye not Agincourt?
> When English slew and hurt
> All their French foemen?
> With our pikes and bills brown
> How the French were beat down,
> Shot by our bowmen.
>
> "Agincourt, Agincourt!
> Know ye not Agincourt?
> English of every sort,
> High men and low men,
> Fought that day wondrous well, as
> All our old stories tell us,
> Thanks to our bowmen.
>
> "Agincourt, Agincourt!
> Know ye not Agincourt?
> When our fifth Harry taught
> Frenchmen to know men,
> And when the day was done
> Thousands then fell to one
> Good English bowman."

So the middle period of the war, like the first period, ends with a great victory for the English, and a flood-time of English success.

Joan of Arc and the Close of the War

Even so great a defeat as this could not make the French princes cease their quarrels. Again the leader of one party was murdered by the follower of another; and the followers of the dead prince became so bitterly hostile that they were willing to join the English against the other party. In this way the Burgundians, as the one party was called, entered into a treaty with Henry of England against the Armagnacs, as the other party was called; and it was agreed that Henry should marry Katherine, the daughter of the insane King, and Henry should become King of France when the old King died. No one seemed to care for the rights of the Dauphin (the French King's son) except the Armagnacs; they, of course, were opposed to all that the Burgundians did.

Both Henry V. of England and poor old Charles VI. of France died within two years after this treaty was signed. Henry had married Katharine as agreed; and though their son (Henry VI.) was a mere baby, only nine months old, he now became King of both England and France. In neither country, however, was his reign to be a happy or a peaceful one. In England the little King's relatives fell to quarreling about the government, just as had happened in France; and when he grew up, like his French grandfather he became insane. At the same time the English found their hold upon France relaxing and the land slipping from their grasp.

Only the Armagnacs at first recognized the Dauphin as King; and for seven years after the death of his father he had great difficulty in keeping any part of France from the hands of the English. In the year 1429, however, a great change took place. A young peasant girl, named Joan of Arc, appeared at the King's court in that year, and under her inspiration and guidance the French cause began to gain, and the English and Burgundian to lose ground.

Joan's home was in the far northeastern part of France, and there she had been brought up in the cottage of her father with her brothers and sisters. There she helped to herd the sheep, assisted her mother in household tasks, and learned to spin and to sew. She never learned to read and write, for that was not thought necessary for peasant girls. Joan was a sweet, good girl, and was very religious. Even in her far-off village the people suffered from the evils which the wars brought upon the land, and Joan's heart was moved by the distress which she saw about her. When she was thirteen she began to hear voices of saints and angels,—of Saint Catherine and Saint Margaret, and of the angel Gabriel. When she was eighteen her "voices" told her that she must go into France, aid the Dauphin, and cause him to be crowned king at Rheims, where the kings of France had been crowned before him.

The cause of the Dauphin at this time was at its lowest ebb. The English were besieging the city of Orleans, on the Loire River; and if that was taken all France would be lost. So the first work of Joan must be to raise the siege of Orleans.

With much difficulty she succeeded in reaching the Dauphin. When she was brought into the room where he was, she picked him out from among all, though she had never seen him, and many of the courtiers were more richly dressed than he. After many weeks she succeeded in persuading his councillors that her "voices" were from God, and not the evil one. Then, at last, she was given a suit of armor, and mounted on a white horse, with a sword at her side and a standard in her hand, she rode at the head of the Dauphin's troops to Orleans.

Joan of Arc and her "voices."

When once Joan had reached that place, she so encouraged the citizens that within eight days the English were forced to raise the siege and retire. It seemed to the French a miracle of God, while the English dreaded and feared her as a witch or sorceress. From this time Joan is called "the Maid of Orleans." Nor did her success stop with the relief of that city. Within a few months, the Dauphin was taken to Rheims, and crowned as true King of France. After this many flocked to his standard who before had taken no part in the war. From that time on the French began to get the advantage of the English; and it was mainly the enthusiasm and faith aroused by the Maid that caused the change.

Joan's work was now almost done. Twice she was wounded while fighting at the head of the King's troops. At last she was taken prisoner by a party of Burgundians, and turned over to the English. By them she was put on trial for heresy and sorcery. She showed much courage and skill before her judges, but she was condemned and sentenced to be burned to death at the stake.

The next day the sentence was carried out. To the last she showed herself brave, kind, and womanly. As the flames mounted about her an Englishman cried out:

"We are lost; we have burned a saint."

Such indeed she was, if a saint was ever made by purity, faith, and noble suffering.

The English burned the Maid and threw her ashes in the river Seine; but they could not undo her work. The French continued to gain victory after victory. Soon the old breach between the Armagnacs and Burgundians was healed, and the Burgundians abandoned the English. Then Paris was gained by the French King. Some years later Normandy was conquered, and finally Aquitaine.

In the year 1453, the long, long war came to an end. Of all the wide territories which the English had once possessed in France, they now held only one little town in the north; and the shadows of a civil war—the War of the Roses—were rising in England to prevent them from ever regaining what they had lost. Down to the time of George III. the English kings continued to style themselves kings of France; but this was a mere form. The French now felt themselves to be a nation, and only a national king could rule over them.

That this was so was mainly due to the Maid of Orleans. She was the real savior of France, and remains its greatest national hero.

End of the Middle Ages

Writers of histories are not agreed as to just when the Middle Ages came to an end; but all unite in saying that the change had come by about the year 1500.

If we ask what this change was, the question is easy to answer, though perhaps hard to understand. When men had come to think different thoughts, and live under different institutions, in the Church and in the State, from those we have been describing, then the end of the Middle Ages had come. Feudalism ceased to be a sufficient tie to bind men together in society, and national states arose. Chivalry ceased to be the noble institution its founders had hoped to make of it and became a picturesque mimicry of high sentiment, without real hold on the life of the time. Men came to rely less upon their guilds and communes, their orders and classes, and act more for themselves as individuals. Ignorance, too, became less dense; and as men learned more of the world, and of themselves, superstition became less universal and degrading.

It was such changes as these that mark the close of the Middle Ages and the beginning of a new time. Many of the events of which we have been reading helped to bring on these changes, and put an end to this period of history.

The Crusades did a great deal, by bringing the different peoples of Europe into contact with one another, and broadening their minds. At the same time, the Crusades helped to develop the commerce which kept the nations in touch, and gave them the wealth needed to encourage art and literature.

The long struggle between the Papacy and the Empire, as we have seen, broke down the power of each, and so prepared the way for the rise of new institutions.

The Hundred Years' War between France and England, by making these nations feel that they *were* French and English, helped to complete the break-up of the old system, and bring in a time when all Europe was divided into a number of national states, each with its own interests and government, and owing obedience to no emperor or other superior.

The capture of Constantinople by the Turks and the fall of the Eastern Empire was another event which helped bring the Middle Ages to a close.

After the Crusades had come to an end, a new branch of Turks, called the Ottomans, had risen to power. In the course of a century and a half, they made themselves masters of all Asia Minor and Palestine, and of a good part of Southeastern Europe as well. At Adrianople, where the Goths had won their first great victory, they fixed their capital; and their "horse-tail" standards were thence borne far up the valley of the Danube, into Hungary and Austria.

For many years the walls of Constantinople proved too much for them, and there the Eastern Empire prolonged its feeble existence. When the Hundred Years' War was just coming to an end, a new sultan came to the throne whose entire energies were devoted to the capture of that city and the making it his capital. In 1453 the attack began. Great cannons,—the largest the world had ever seen,—now thundered away, along with catapults, battering-rams, and other engines which the Middle Ages used.

After fifty-three days, the city was taken. Then the Christian churches became Mohammedan mosques; and the standard of the Sultans floated where for a thousand years had hung the banner of the Eastern Emperors. In this way was established the Ottoman Empire, the continued existence of which causes some of the hardest problems which the Christian nations have to face to-day.

To escape from Turkish rule, great numbers of Greek scholars fled from Constantinople to the West, bringing with them their knowledge of the Greek tongue, and great quantities of Greek manuscripts.

All these events which we have been recounting helped to bring the Middle Ages to a close; but other things helped even more than these. One was what we call the Revival of Learning; another was certain great inventions which the later Middle Ages produced; and a third was the discovery of new lands and new peoples across the seas.

Although the monks had done much for learning during the Middle Ages, nevertheless a great deal of the knowledge and literature of the olden time had disappeared. Many of the most famous works of the old Greek and Latin authors had been lost sight of altogether. Others, also, which the monks had, they did not understand; and still others they almost feared to read because they were full of the stories of the old gods, whom the Middle Ages regarded as evil spirits. The Latin, too, which the monks spoke and wrote was very incorrect and corrupt; and practically no one outside of the Eastern Empire understood Greek at all.

About the beginning of the fourteenth century, however, men began to take a new interest in the old literature. They began to write more correct Latin. They searched for forgotten manuscripts which might contain some of the lost works. They corrected and edited the manuscripts they had, and began to make dictionaries and grammars to aid them in understanding them. Soon some began even to learn Greek, and collect Greek manuscripts as well as Latin ones.

Above all, scholars tried to put themselves back in the place of the old Greeks and Romans, and look at the world through their eyes, and not through the eyes of the medieval monks.

The result was that many things began to seem different to them. They no longer feared this world as the monks had done. They took delight in its beauty, and no longer thought that everything which was pleasant was therefore sinful. And because they believed that man's life as a human being was good in itself, the new scholars were called "humanists," and their studies and ways of thinking "humanism."

This change in the way of thinking came only gradually, and it was a hundred years before humanism began to spread from Italy, where it first arose, to the countries north of the Alps. But then the Germans contributed something which helped to spread humanism more rapidly. This was the invention of printing.

The making of books, by forming each letter in each copy, separately with the pen, was so slow that men had long hunted for some means of lessening the labor. They found that by engraving the page upon a block of wood, and printing from this, they could make a hundred copies almost as easily as one, so in the fifteenth century "block books," as they were called, began to be made. But the trouble with these

Early printers

was that every page had to be engraved separately, and this proved such a task that only books of a very few pages were made in this way.

Then it occurred to John Gutenberg, of Strasburg, that if he made the letters *separate*, he could use the same ones over and over again to form new pages; and if instead of cutting the letters themselves, he made *moulds* to produce them, then he could cast his type in metal (which would be better than wood anyway), and from the one mould he could make as many of each letter as was necessary.

In this way printing from movable metal types was invented by Gutenberg, about the year 1450. It seems like a very small thing when we tell about it, but it was one of the most important inventions that the world has ever seen.

The first book that was printed was the Bible, in Latin. Soon presses and printing offices were established all over Western Europe, printing Bibles and other books, and selling them so cheaply that almost every one could now afford to buy. The invention of printing thus served to spread humanism and the knowledge of the Bible throughout Europe, and these two together brought on the Reformation and helped put an end entirely to the Middle Ages.

The introduction of gunpowder was also, in the end, of very great importance.

Nobody knows just when or by whom gunpowder was invented; but it was used to make rockets and fireworks in India and China long before it was known in Europe. In the fourteenth century the Moors of Spain introduced the use of cannon into Europe; and by the date of the battle of Crecy (1346) cannon were to be found in

Early cannon

most of the western countries. These, however, were usually small, and were often composed merely of iron staves roughly hooped together, or even of wood or of leather; and the powder used was weak and without sufficient force to throw the ball any great distance.

It was not gunpowder, as is sometimes said, that first overthrew the armored knight of the Middle Ages; it was the archers who did this, and the foot-soldiers armed with long pikes for thrusting, and with halberds hooked at the end by means of which the knight might be pulled from his horse.

As the cannon were improved, however, they became of great service in breaking down the walls of feudal castles, and of hostile cities; and so, in the end, they helped greatly to change the mode of making war. But it was not until the Middle Ages had quite come to an end that gunpowder had become so useful in small hand guns that the old long-bows and crossbows completely disappeared.

Two other inventions that came into use in the Middle Ages were also of great importance in bringing in the new time. These were the compass, or magnetic needle, and the "cross-staff" used by sailors for finding latitude.

Like gunpowder, the compass came from Asia, where it was used by the Chinese long before the birth of Christ. It was introduced into Europe as a guide to sailors about the beginning of the fourteenth century. It enabled them to steer steadily in whatever direction they wished, even when far from land; but it could not tell them where they were at any given time.

The cross-staff did this in part, for it could tell them their latitude by measuring the height of the north star above the horizon. The "astrolabe" was another instrument which was used for the same purpose. These were very ancient instruments, but they did not begin to be used by sailors until some time in the fifteenth century. Even then the sailor had to trust to guess-work for his longitude, for the watches and chronometers by which ship captains now measure longitude were not yet invented; and sailing maps were only beginning to be made.

The cross-staff

Yet, in spite of these disadvantages, and in spite of the smallness of the vessels, and the terrors of unknown seas, great progress was made in the discovery of new lands before the close of our period. The commerce of the Italian cities made their citizens skillful sailors, voyaging up and down the Mediterranean and even beyond the straits of Gibraltar. The Normans and certain of the Spanish peoples, early sailed boldly into the northern and western seas.

But it was the little state of Portugal that led the way in the discovery of new worlds. A prince of that state gave so much attention to discovery in the first half of the fifteenth century, that he was called Prince Henry "the Navigator." Under his wise direction Portuguese seamen began working their way south along the coast of Africa. In this way the Madeira and Canary Islands, the Azores, and Cape Verde were discovered one after another before 1450; and after Prince Henry's death, a Portuguese captain succeeded in 1486 in reaching the southernmost point of Africa, to which the Portuguese King gave the name "Cape of Good Hope." Twelve years later, in 1498, Vasco da Gama realized this hope by reaching the East Indies, and so opened up communication by sea with India.

Six years before, as we all know, Columbus while trying to reach the same region by sailing westward, discovered the new world of America,—though he died thinking that he had reached Asia and the East Indies.

So we come to a time when Europe had emerged from the darkness of the Middle Ages, and was preparing, first, to make a reformation in religion, and then to go forth and found new Europes across the seas. But the details of these events belong to the story of Modern Times, and not to the Middle Ages. To complete our story we need only tell what was the condition of each of the principal states of Europe at this time, and point out the part it was to play in the new period.

Germany was the country which was to take the lead in bringing about the Reformation in religion. Its people were more serious-minded than the peoples south of the Alps, and felt more keenly the evils in the Church; above all, it was there that the great reformer, Martin Luther, was born. But Germany was split up into a great many little states, each with its own prince or king, and each practically independent of the Emperor. So there was no national strength in Germany; and when the movement began to establish colonies and take possession of the New World, Germany took no part.

Italy also was too much split up among rival cities and warring principalities to take any part in colonization; and the Eastern nations, such as Russia and Poland, were not used to the sea. Sweden for a while became very powerful in the seventeenth century, owing to the ability of its great King, Gustavus Adolphus, and it established colonies on the river Delaware. The Dutch also for a time became a great seafaring people, and established colonies on the banks of the Hudson. Both these countries, however, soon lost their strength, and their colonies, for the most part, passed into the hands of larger and stronger nations.

It was the nations of Western Europe,—England, France, and Spain,—that were to take the lead in building up new Europes across the water.

England at the close of the Middle Ages was just coming out of the long War of the Roses which was mentioned in the last chapter. That war had brought Henry VII., the grandfather of the great Queen Elizabeth, to the throne; and under him England was strong, united and prosperous. Thus when the Venetian, John Cabot, asked King Henry for ships to sail westward to the lands newly found by Columbus, his request was granted. In that way the beginning was made of a claim which, after many years, gave the English the possession of all the eastern part of North America.

France also was strong, united, and prosperous at the close of the Middle Ages. Through several centuries the kings had been busy breaking down the influence of the great nobles, and gathering the power into their own hands. So France was ready to take part in the exploration and settlement of the New World. The result was that the French got Canada and Louisiana, and for a while it seemed as though the whole of the great Mississippi basin was about to pass into their hands.

It was Spain, however, that was to take the chief part in the work of making known the New World to the Old, and in establishing there the first colonies.

From the days when the Moors came into Spain in 711, the Spanish Christians had been occupied for nearly eight hundred years in defending themselves in the mountains against the Mohammedans and in winning back, bit by bit, the land which the Goths had lost. Little by little, new states had there arisen—Castile, Leon, Aragon, and Portugal. Next these states began to unite—Leon with Castile, and then (by the marriage of Isabella to Ferdinand) Castile with Aragon. In the year 1492, the last of the Moors were overcome, and the whole peninsula, except Portugal alone, was united under one king and queen.

Thus Spain, too, was made strong, united, and prosperous; and was prepared, with the confidence of victory upon it, to send forth Columbus, Vespucius, De Soto, Cortez, and Magellan, to lay the foundations of the first great colonial empire.

All this was made possible by the Middle Ages. The blending of the old Germans with the peoples of the Roman Empire, that made the Spaniards, the French, and, to a certain extent, the English people. The events of the Middle Ages that shaped their development, and formed the strong national monarchies which alone could colonize the New World. And it was the institutions and ideas, which had been shaped and formed and re-shaped and re-formed in the Middle Ages, that the colonists brought with them from across the sea.

So, in a way, the story of the Middle Ages is a part of our own history. The New World influenced the Old World a very great deal; but it was itself influenced yet more largely by the older one.

Lightning Source UK Ltd.
Milton Keynes UK
UKHW010644051022
409964UK00001B/144